THE
JESUS
QUESTION

The
Jesus
Question

by

J. A. Ziesler

Lutterworth Press · Guildford and London

First published 1980

By the same author:
The Meaning of Righteousness in Paul
Christian Asceticism

ISBN 0 7188 2431 8

200146716

232

Set in 11/12pt. Times
Printed and bound in Great Britain by
Fakenham Press Limited,
Fakenham, Norfolk

Contents

Acknowledgements

I am indebted to several of my colleagues for informal discussion and information, but in a more substantial way to Professor Kenneth Grayston and Dr Denys Turner, both of whom made detailed comments on an earlier draft of this book. For a number of specific points I owe them my thanks and I hope they will accept this in place of item by item acknowledgement. They have saved me from errors and inaccuracies, and if indeed many such still remain, these are doubtless where I have ignored their advice. I am also indebted to my wife for her practical help in producing an intelligible typescript.

The excerpt from the 'Secret Gospel' in chapter 2 is taken from the translation by Professor F. F. Bruce in *The 'Secret' Gospel of Mark*, published in 1974 by the Athlone Press. I am very grateful both to Professor Bruce and the Press for permission to quote it here.

Introduction

'Thank God for Jesus' says the sticker in the window of the car down my street. It is astonishing how in a supposedly post-Christian age the figure of Jesus is more inescapable than ever. It is only to be expected that the churches should talk about him endlessly, but what is not so expected is that he should be a focus of attention in many different ways and among quite different groups of people outside the churches. The musical, *Jesus Christ Superstar*, has broken all records in London, and plays and especially books about him continue to appear in intimidating numbers written sometimes by friends, sometimes by foes, and often by those who wish to explain to their own satisfaction what he was 'really' like. There seems to be a compulsion driving those who reject formal Christianity none the less to account for Jesus, to find a place for him in their own scheme of things, and to explain what he really intended. They seem unable simply to ignore him.

Christians, of course, pour out books about him by the thousand – some works of technical scholarship, some little more than pious romanticism, quite a lot somewhere in between. Sporadically there is controversy about him as traditional doctrines are rigorously questioned and then vigorously defended, and often (as recently) one of the doctrines near the centre of the debate is the doctrine of the 'incarnation', i.e. the belief that in Jesus Christ we find God-become-man. Is this myth, or truth, or both? Much of the recent debate was sparked off by a book called *The Myth of God Incarnate* (1977) to which we must return later on, but sparks have little effect on the undergrowth unless it is already tinder-dry, and at least in England it was.

For almost any variety of Christianity the figure of Jesus is

1

crucial. His teaching is important but not central, for while its balance and emphasis, the way it fits together, may be unparalleled, its content does have parallels elsewhere, especially in Rabbinic Judaism. His miracles and his noble character also have their parallels, even within the Bible to some extent, and he is not the only great religious leader to have suffered unjustly and to have been killed. No, if they are wise, Christians do not claim that Jesus was unique in every respect, but rather that he is the centre, the fixed point around which everything revolves, the standpoint from which God, man, the self, and the world are to be understood.

For Christians of all sorts, the heart of their faith is 'christology' (shorthand for the understanding of what and who Christ is), but there still remains the question of *what* christology. The picture of Jesus comes in innumerable varieties, and even in traditional piety the range of understandings is wide. In this book, I shall not be attempting anything novel, but shall try to make some important issues clear, disentangle some threads in contemporary arguments, and show some methods of working in the study of Jesus. The purpose is strictly introductory, and the further reading suggested for each topic is an important next step.

Three Questions

Our discussion will concentrate on three areas.

1. The question of history: how much do we really know about Jesus, and how much do we need to know for the purposes of Christian faith?
2. The question of what the New Testament says: does it always say the same thing, and does it say what the creeds of the church say?
3. The question of interpretation: times, conceptions, world-views and meanings of words all change, so what must modern man now say in order to convey what was meant by ancient words?

Although these questions are closely linked, they are separate, and it may help to look at them in turn, even if we know that in the end we cannot keep them apart.

Approaching the Questions

One way of tackling questions like these, which can for some be painful or even shocking, is that of relying on experience or dogma or both. Christ is divine, we may say, because I experience him as God, because the Bible says he is divine, and because the church has always said so. I believe the Bible conveys God's truth reliably, and I trust the tradition of the church, so there is nothing more to discuss. If modern scholars find difficulties, this shows that their grasp of God's truth is faulty. Now this can seem an impregnable position, and there are those within the churches who adopt it deliberately or tacitly (just as there are dogmatic atheists who adopt its exact opposite). The result is that the whole matter lies outside the realm of discussion.

The approach which we shall adopt, however, is that of examining all the questions with as open a mind as possible, running the risk of not finding the 'right' answers, or of having to change our minds about some things, or of becoming less certain than we were about others. In other words, we shall use the methods of critical scholarship and historical enquiry. The risk that this entails is well illustrated by a veto placed by G. A. Wells against all talk about a real Jesus, and we must face this before going any further.

A Decisive Veto?

Over the years there have been many attempts to argue that Jesus never existed, but rather is a mythical cult-figure, akin perhaps to Cybele or Mithras, about whom for some reason pseudo-historical stories began to gather. This led finally to our gospels, which are works of historical fiction. Christian scholars have in return argued that such reasonings are weak, fallacious, or perverse, and that the existence of Jesus of

3

Nazareth, crucified under Pontius Pilate, is one of the best attested facts of ancient history. It is widely assumed that the question is now closed. When, therefore, Wells (who is a professor of German) revives the old arguments and adds new ones, he tends to be ignored or summarily dismissed. Nevertheless his books are serious works, especially the second one, *Did Jesus Exist?* (1975), and require a serious response, for he is neither a mere polemicist nor ignorant of modern biblical study. Moreover, he writes with a restraint and courtesy which some of his Christian reviewers would do well to match. He firmly obliges us to consider again the strength of the evidence for the very existence of Jesus.

In the end, his case rests on a few awkward facts.

1. In Paul's letters, the earliest surviving Christian documents, there is little (nothing, says Wells) to require that Jesus be a figure of the recent past. Apart from the death and resurrection, virtually no reference is made to Jesus' life on earth, and in any case there is no hint of date. This is because Jesus was originally a dying-and-rising-god figure, and not historic at all. Passages like Philippians 2 which can be taken to refer to his character (humility in this case) should rather be referred to his mythical descent from, and ascent to, heaven. The 'appearances' in 1 Corinthians 15 are mystical, and do not imply that the Jesus who appeared had recently, indeed ever, been on earth. Wells has more difficulties with 1 Corinthians 11, the story of the Last Supper, but after considering and rejecting the possibility of interpolation, he decides it is a story devised to explain a ritual, the church's eucharist. He can thus maintain that Paul was ignorant of an earthly Jesus, that he probably thought Jesus to have lived some time in the remote past, though he doubtless did (wrongly) suppose there once was such a person.

2. Wells accepts that there is evidence for Jesus outside Christian sources, notably in the Roman historian Tacitus, in the Jewish historian Josephus, and in the writings of the Rabbis. All these, however, fall before his critical axe. He rightly dates the Rabbinic materials well after the alleged time of Jesus, and not unreasonably sees them as telling us more

4

about Christian–Jewish controversy from the 2nd century onwards than about Jesus. They are anti-Christian propaganda, not historical reminiscence. Like many others, he thinks the very few, very brief references in Josephus are Christian interpolations. As for Tacitus, who wrote about 120 AD, and who records that Jesus had been executed under Pontius Pilate in the reign of Tiberius, Wells argues that by this time Christians themselves honestly believed this, and that the Roman merely echoes their own view of their origins. Tacitus would not, he thinks, bother to check the official records. No contemporary evidence for the existence of Jesus survives scrutiny. (John the Baptist is a different matter.)

3. The church's gospels, he believes, are poor evidence. None of them is to be dated before the end of the first century AD, not even Mark. Other writings, e.g. 1 Timothy 6:13, which do not locate an historical Jesus in the time of Pilate, all date from not earlier than the end of the first century. It is not until about 100 AD that an historical figure from the time of Pilate begins to emerge.

4. For some reason about this time, the figure of Jesus moved out of myth and into history. This seems odd, for in the contemporary world pagan religions valued history rather little – it scarcely mattered whether their gods and goddesses had ever lived on earth or not. Why should Christianity be different? The answer Wells gives is complex and has several stages, but he does not accuse the early Christians of deliberate fraud. Much of the 'biography' of Jesus was constructed from Old Testament models, e.g. many of the details of the passion story reflect motifs from various psalms, especially Psalm 22. They do indeed, and many scholars agree that they were told in order to direct the reader to the Old Testament models, but Wells believes that the whole story was entirely constructed from such materials. He argues that as a general rule, religious rituals precede the myths which arise later to give them coherence and explanation, and in the present case, the passion story arose to explain the eucharist (not *vice versa!*). Larger construction blocks were also used, of course –

5

elements from Gnosticism, from the 'mystery religions', and from Jewish messianism. Influential messianic ideas included those of a messiah who would rise from the dead together with others (2 Esdras 7), and a literal reading of the descent to earth of personified divine 'wisdom' (Wisdom of Solomon 7 and 9 – this and 2 Esdras are both in the Apocrypha to the Old Testament). The reason why Jesus develops into a figure of the *recent* past is that the Qumran Essenes, the Dead Sea Scrolls sect, had their great 'Teacher of Righteousness' who had lived perhaps a century earlier. By some sort of contagion, Christians began to see their great Teacher in comparable chronological terms.

Obviously I have ignored matters on which Wells spends much time – the explanation of undoubted historical difficulties, inconsistencies and improbabilities in the gospel accounts. For all this, and for his arguments against those who reject his theories, it is necessary to read his books.

Responding to the Veto

Many of Wells' points are valid, and many of his positions are defensible. The gospels, for instance, could be as late as he thinks, though it is extremely unlikely. Paul's silence about the life, character, and teaching of Jesus is distinctly strange, and cannot easily be brushed aside. Wells' treatment of Tacitus is disputable, as is that of Josephus, but these are not knock-down arguments which enable us quickly to dispose of him. So how are we to respond?

1. We can say that the New Testament is divinely inspired, that therefore Wells is culpably wrong, and that debate with such an unbeliever is pointless.

2. We can say that what Wells is trying to do is irrelevant to Christianity correctly understood. Even if Wells should prove right, the Christ of faith is alive and active, is our window on God, and illuminates us, not because of something that may have been true (or not) hundreds of years ago, but because his illumination answers our needs. At the end of *Did Jesus*

Exist? Wells says that this is the response he expects from Christian theologians.

3. We can engage him on his own historical ground, and see where the argument leads, running the risk that he may have the better of it.

I shall return to the first, and especially to the second, of these responses in the next chapter, but meanwhile wish to attempt the third. For the sake of argument, let us grant him his datings, however improbable they may be, and his rejection of Tacitus and Josephus. It is what he does with Paul and in particular with 1 Corinthians 11 and 15 that is the nub of the matter.

1 Corinthians 11:23–26 (The Last Supper)
This purports to describe a real event, on the eve of the death of Jesus. How long ago it was is not specified, but real happenings and real people seem to be intended. Wells, as we have seen, thinks it is a story formed by the church to explain its own ritual practice, the eucharist, and nothing more. Paul, writing in the middle of the first century, is unaware that this event never happened because Jesus never existed. He (Paul) thinks it all happened in the remote past. Wells also thinks that 'on the night on which he was betrayed' refers not to Judas, but to Jesus' being delivered up to death (the Greek word is ambiguous: 'betray' and 'deliver up' are both possible meanings). He could be right, though it is not probable, and in any case this is a side issue. The main question is whether Paul thought it all happened a long time ago.

Against Wells, it seems from Galatians 1:17 that Paul knows that Christianity is new, and the same emerges from 1 Corinthians 15 as we shall see. *If Paul did know that the Christian faith had only lately appeared, he ought to have known also that it was based on a myth of dying and rising, not on an historical occurrence*, assuming Wells is right. Moreover, it would be extraordinary if Paul should be talking about an event in the distant past, and give no indication of the gap between that event and the religion belatedly based

7

upon it. Yet if Wells is right, Paul's ignorance of the non-existence of Jesus can be explained only by supposing such a gap.

1 Corinthians 15:1–9 (Resurrection Appearances)
Wells does not deny that Paul and others had visionary experiences which they (erroneously) interpreted as appearances of the risen Christ, but argues that nothing in this passage need mean that the cross and resurrection were recent. The experiences were recent, but Paul and the others must have imagined they were the reflection of long-ago events – in reality, says Wells, there were no original events at all. It is only the visions which need to be placed within Paul's lifetime, and only they which need to be regarded as actual, if misinterpreted, events. Perhaps the visions had only recently started, or perhaps Paul mentions only recent ones. At all events, there is no closeness in time between the 'appearances' and the supposed happenings they reflect.

I do not think the passage can properly be read this way. 'On the third day' (v. 4) may be a conventional indication of time, influenced by the Old Testament, but it scarcely allows years, decades, or centuries between death and resurrection. Again, there is no indication of gap between resurrection and the first appearance to Cephas. Rapid sequence is inescapable, and the rapid sequence must therefore *all* have happened in Paul's own lifetime if the last item, the appearances, did. In short, while there is not a lot in Paul that anchors the Jesus story to a particular recent time, *there is enough*.

Theory of Origins
Syncretistic religious creations are not unknown, and we cannot too quickly rule out Wells' theory. Yet the whole development is supposed to have happened in a very short space of time. Within a century at most, a dying-and-rising-god myth has turned into a full blown, very Jewish, historical religion, complete with marked varieties, Markan, Lukan, Matthaean, and Johannine. This is remarkable. Equally strik-

ing is the fact that almost no traces of mythical origin remain in the gospels, even in the passion story. If the myth is there to underpin the ritual, and the history is just a development of the myth, it is distinctly odd that in one of the gospels, John, the ritual (eucharist) is not directly mentioned at all. Indeed all the gospels, on Wells' theory, are strangely and inexplicably lacking in direct explanation of the death of Jesus. It is almost as if the writers have forgotten why they were writing – to underpin a ritual.

It is hard to believe that Wells gives an adequate explanation of the gospels as we have them. Surely they ought to look rather different, if he is right? Why have so much about the life *and teaching* of this dying-and-rising-figure, if all that really matters is the death, and the resurrection, in which the initiate can share? And how could this enormous switch have happened so quickly? Wells can cite parallel cases where myths have been turned into history, but the time-scale is usually vast, and the 'history' is not very important anyway, whereas in Christianity it is the very centre.

It is not really odd that there is little about Jesus in contemporary Jewish and pagan writing. For a long time the Christians were a small and obscure body, and even at the time of Jesus, events that were earth-shaking for believers doubtless seemed unimportant in the world of great affairs, even Jewish great affairs. In the end, Wells is not persuasive. The veto can be overridden, and we may proceed. Yet nagging doubts remain. Were we bound to come to this conclusion because of faith, prejudice, or bigotry? What would happen to Christianity if Wells could prove his case so that no rational man could disagree? In other words, how important is history to Christianity?

Notes on Books

M. Martin, *Jesus Now*, E. P. Dutton, New York, 1973, and Collins, 1975, gives a high-spirited account of some of the many pictures of Jesus.

John Hick (ed.), *The Myth of God Incarnate*, SCM Press, 1977 – a controversial symposium expressing difficulty about traditional Christian language, especially about the divinity of Christ. Henceforth referred to as *Myth*.

G. A. Wells, *The Jesus of the Early Christians*, Pemberton, 1971. There is little point in reading this, for the author was ignorant of much modern scientific study of the Bible, and consequently tried to maintain some very weak positions. He later brought himself up to date with remarkable speed, and his resulting second book, *Did Jesus Exist?* Elek/Pemberton, 1975, is much more plausible. Everything one needs to know about his views can be read here.

H. G. Wood, *Did Christ Really Live?* SCM Press, 1938, is an old but still readable reply to earlier attacks on the historicity of Jesus. The precise targets, however, are now forgotten.

I
The Question of History

1. Can we know what Jesus was like?

For about 200 years, there has been a growing suspicion that the real, historical Jesus was quite a different person from the Lord venerated by the church. The New Testament and the church's tradition give – or so it is feared – an idealized and theologized portrait which obscures the man as he actually was. The question is how much do we know about him, in the same historical sense that we know about Julius Caesar or George Washington. We know what the church has believed about him, but is that the same thing? A further question of concern to Christians is how much historical knowledge we *need* for belief in Jesus Christ. These two questions, how much we know, and how much we need to know, are closely tied together in much recent thinking about Jesus as an historical figure.

There have been three different sorts of answer to this double-barrelled question, or so it appears from some work done by Harvey K. McArthur, and we shall follow his suggestion.

Answer 1: Historical Certainty

This view is that Christian faith needs a firm historical underpinning, and that in fact it has it. It is important that the Christ in whom Christians believe should be continuous with the man who once walked the streets of Jerusalem, except of course that the Christ of faith is a risen, ascended, glorified and reigning figure, and thus a *transformed* Jesus. Allowing for this, there is complete continuity between the Jesus of history and the Christ of faith. Where do we obtain the assurance of this continuity? Not always from historical research, though sometimes this plays a part. More usually, there is a prior belief in the inspiration of the Bible, so that we know Jesus must have been as depicted in the gospels simply because God speaks through the Bible and it is unthinkable that it should be erroneous in any matter of substance. The same sort of reliance may be placed on the tradition of the church, or on religious experience – if I have some kind of encounter with Christ through reading the New Testament, I am not likely to question its historical reliability.

The historical certainty answer thus relies on something other than historical enquiry, though scholars who hold this view may well none the less engage in historical research, in the confidence that though it may not always support their faith, it can never destroy it either. This answer is probably tacitly given by multitudes of Christians. Those who reject it tend to suspect that its exponents will ignore overwhelming historical probability rather than admit that some element in the New Testament picture of Jesus is inauthentic. Yet it is a strong position so long as the prior faith in Bible or church, or the confidence in religious experience, is maintained.

Some who are firmly attached to the New Testament picture of Christ, feel under no obligation to such later formularies as the Nicene Creed and the Definition of Chalcedon. Others, especially in the Catholic tradition, regard such formularies as being authoritative for them, and therefore as still saying what ought to be said about Christ, despite needing translation into modern words and categories. For both groups, there is complete continuity between the Jesus of history and the Christ of the church's faith. We need historical certainty, and we have it.

Answer 2: Historical Immunity

This is the opposite view. We know very little with historical certainty, but it matters not in the least. Faith is faith, and therefore cannot depend on the vagaries of historical enquiry, i.e. it is immune to historical questioning. Some have gone so far as to say that Christ's significance is independent of what he was like and even of whether he ever existed. He functions

14

as a powerful symbol, and the test of Christian truth has nothing to do with history, but only with how one's own life, one's relationships, and the world, are illuminated by the figure of Christ. On this view, Wells could be completely right, and yet it would make no difference to Christianity, properly understood.

More commonly, however, it is agreed that a minimum of historical grounding is needed, that we need to know that Jesus lived, was rejected, and was finally executed. The most famous exponent of this view was Rudolf Bultmann. As a Christian existentialist, he was concerned above all with the individual, subjective response of a person to life's challenges, decisions, anxieties, and insecurities, and to the proclamation of the Christian gospel. Concern with the objective world (i.e., outside and neutral to the person) and with such matters as the end of the cosmos or what exactly happened in Galilee or Jerusalem in 30 AD, is apt to distract attention from what really matters. It is not just that we *can* know little about such matters – it is rather that we ought not to want to know, for these concerns lead us away from faith. If something matters, it cannot matter abstractly, but must matter *to* someone. The subjective is therefore the important. If the Christian gospel is true, it must be true for persons who respond to it and live by it. 'Objective' or 'historical' truth is irrelevant. Whether the resurrection happened in Jerusalem 'objectively' is unimportant; what matters totally is whether it happens in my existence.

Bultmann sharpens this by his use of two different German words for 'history'. He uses one (*Historie*) to mean bare facts of the past – the sort of history we call 'dead' meaning that it is remote from and irrelevant to us and our concerns. He uses another (*Geschichte*) for history that is alive because it comes out of the past to meet us, history that at some point touches our lives and affects our understanding of ourselves. That something happened, whether true or not, is insignificant unless it impinges in some way on someone. On the other hand, what does impinge on someone, illuminate someone's life and self-understanding, is *Geschichte* whether or not it actually happened. What did or did not happen long ago is unimportant compared to its effect on me, now. So far as Jesus Christ is concerned, what matters is his effect on my life and self-understanding now; his reality and decisiveness are independent of what happened in 30 AD, and of whether the gospel stories are true, and of whether Jesus was as tradition pictures him. All that is necessary is that Jesus should have really lived and been rejected and died.

Indeed, historical enquiry is irrelevant to faith, except in so far as it removes false historical props on which we are tempted to rely. *Evidence is the enemy of faith.* Remove evidence, and faith can operate. Bultmann thus combines what looks like total historical scepticism with what looks like a simple evangelical faith, and this latter point can be seen most clearly in his published sermons.

Clearly there are problems about this 'immune from historical enquiry' position. For one thing, it requires an existentialist philosophical standpoint which exalts the subjective and deprecates the objective, and this has never had the impact in Britain that it had in continental Europe. Even in Europe and in the United States its influence is now greatly diminished from its post-war flowering. Bultmann's kind of Christianity fails to answer to modern interest in the community (not just the church community) and the cosmos, in other words in the world outside the individual's subjectivity. Moreover, not even many radical critics really believe that we have as little solid historical information about Jesus as Bultmann would like.

Perhaps the strongest objection is also the hardest to state. When I respond to the proclamation of Christ that liberates me, what am I responding to? What *content* does the name 'Christ' convey? How do I know I am not being converted to something evil, or narrow, or silly? What is to stop a variety of Christs taking the field, a Fascist Christ, a left-wing guerrilla Christ, a middle-class suburban Christ, a libertine Christ, a legalistic Christ, and so on? Men do indeed fashion Christ after their own wishes, at least to some extent, but is that to be condoned, and is there no control? Does the response correspond to any outside reality at all? Unless there is some control, and the main control must be historical, we cannot discuss christology at all, for it would be like the game of croquet in *Through the Looking Glass* – no fixed points, nothing standing still. If discussion is to be meaningful, there must be some continuity between the Jesus of history and the Christ of faith. This necessity has greatly exercised Bultmann's pupils who have tended to modify his historical scepticism and his rejection of the value of historical data. Yet it can still be said (as by G. Bornkamm in the introduction to his notable book, *Jesus of Nazareth*) that faith is and must be independent of the vicissitudes of historical research. Like that of historical certainty, the idea of historical immunity has a lasting attractiveness.

Answer 3: Historical Risk

Those who give this answer accept that Christian faith is at least partly vulnerable and exposed to historical enquiry. They do not consider that we have historical certainty, nor that Christianity is immune to critical historical investigation. If someone were to prove with overwhelming probability that Jesus never existed, or had been a quite different character (a libertine magician, for example – see the next chapter), and that the primitive church had falsified the picture, their Christianity would collapse. Historical research cannot create faith, but it could destroy it. This is because faith is essentially a going *beyond* the evidence, not a going *against* it. Once show that the evidence is incompatible with faith, e.g. by discovering that Jesus really had been a libertine magician, then faith becomes irrational and absurd. There is a clear risk; something could be discovered to make faith impossible for any reasonable person.

Exponents of this view maintain that it fits the nature of Christian belief, which is that God works not unambiguously or like a juggernaut, but precisely in and through a human life that was largely ignored, rejected, and misunderstood. A risk-taking God requires a risk-taking faith. None the less they usually consider that in fact there is continuity between the Jesus of the historians and the Christ of the believers. It does turn out that historical enquiry provides us with a Jesus congruous with the Christ venerated by the church. There are various ways of stating this, for as we saw in the first answer, the two cannot simply be equated. Jesus of Nazareth was not the exalted Lord of the world while still walking about the hills of Galilee; he became that after his resurrection and exaltation. One way is to say with E. Käsemann that what was *implicit* in the Jesus of history becomes *explicit* in Christian faith. Even Bultmann provides some continuity by saying that the Proclaimer becomes the Proclaimed, in other words that while Jesus preached the kingdom of God, the church preaches Jesus. The preacher is now the one who is preached.

It is possible that in all these answers we have accepted a wrong way of putting the question, and that by setting up two distinct figures, the Jesus of history and the Christ of faith, we exacerbate the problem. Having pulled them apart, we then must find ways of reuniting them, but in reality no one supposes there are two such distinct figures. Perhaps a better way of putting the matter is to say that we are trying to reconcile what Jesus is, as the church's Lord and Christ, with what he was, as an historical person.

How much do we really know?

This question is particularly crucial to those who adopt the third position above. During the 50s and 60s, much scholarly energy was expended in trying, by strictly historical methods, to learn how much could be established about Jesus, an enterprise which has been dubbed 'The New Quest of the Historical Jesus'. Bultmann viewed it with grave suspicion, but nevertheless his pupils were heavily involved in it. The name comes from the title of a notable book by Albert Schweitzer, *The Quest of the Historical Jesus*, published in German in 1906, and in English in 1910, in which he reviewed 19th-century liberal lives of Jesus, and showed dramatically that scholars had found what they expected to find. In attempting to portray Jesus freed from the theological barnacles gathered as the Jesus-tradition passed through the church, they presented instead a mirror-image of their own ideals. They found not the Jesus of history, but Jesus as they liked to think of him. No doubt everyone does this, but it must not be passed off as historical research, and Schweitzer showed that this had been happening, all unintentionally. His own view was that Jesus was a stranger to our ideals and preoccupations, an eschatological prophet, i.e. one announcing the 'End' of the present order, who died mistaken and disappointed.

The *new* 'Quest' tries to learn from the mistakes of the old, and begins by accepting that all New Testament books are documents of faith and commitment, not unbiased sources. Even the supposedly straightforward Mark is a product of theology and of commitment to Christ, a work of faith like the other gospels. Does this make it useless as a source of hard historical information? How can we tell where history ends and faith begins? It is always a delicate matter to distinguish between the two. To take a stock example: 'Jesus died on the cross' – that is history that can be discussed, and the evidence concerning it assessed, in just the same way that we can discuss Hannibal's crossing the Alps with his elephants; 'Jesus died for me' – that is a matter of faith, not history, for we are now talking about divine purpose, which can never be the subject of historical enquiry. It is a matter of interpretation, a matter of belief. Yet it may not be as simple as this example suggests, for the two, history and faith, may be too deeply interpenetrated to be separated. It is not a question of there being a layer of interpretation on top of a layer of fact, like icing on a cake. An untheological account of Jesus never existed, for merely by selecting certain things to tell about him, and ignoring others, a process of theological interpretation is at work. All 'facts' are a mixture of what happened and how it was understood. Despite this, however, some scholars in recent decades have not been discouraged, and have worked out methods by which gospel material can be tested.

Criteria of Authenticity
The most famous test for discovering hard (i.e. incontrovert-

ible) fact in the gospels is the so-called 'criterion of dissimilarity', which goes something like this,

> If a story or a saying appears not to reflect the interests and beliefs of the early church, nor to reflect current Jewish interests and beliefs, then on purely historical grounds it may be held to be authentic (i.e. it goes back to Jesus himself).

This is intended to be a strictly historical procedure, nothing to do with faith, or at least not dependent on faith.

Obviously there is much gospel material in complete accord with the faith of the early church, and which could therefore originate from it. There is also much that fits contemporary Judaism, and could originate there. The historian must concede both these points, though of course *could* is not the same as *did*, a distinction some critics apparently overlook. All that has been established is that this saying or that story cannot be shown to be authentic; it has not necessarily been shown to be inauthentic. Nevertheless the historian cannot safely work with this material; what he needs is what escapes the net, what survives the application of the criterion, and what can thus be claimed as *demonstrably* authentic.

Other criteria are proposed and used by many scholars: multiple attestation (i.e. occurring in several sources or in several different sorts of material), and semitic colouring (i.e. clearly from a Palestinian setting), are two examples. Yet it is the criterion of dissimilarity which is crucial. Is it foolproof? Some think not. For one thing, if applied rigorously nothing at all would get through, because everything in the gospels reflects early Christian faith in one way or another, and everything in the life of Jesus reflects current Judaism in one way or another. In practice, however, some things are held to be compatible with, but not characteristic of, early Christianity or contemporary Judaism, and so to escape the net. Some critics argue that there is historical risk even in using the criterion, because we know too little about both early Christianity and contemporary Judaism to use it effectively. More seriously still, some argue that using the criterion leaves us with a distorted picture of Jesus – with everything removed which linked him to his followers and to his socio-religious environment. The criterion leads us to the unique, but the *characteristic* is what we need to know.

Despite this, it is claimed that using the criterion can establish some important matters with a high degree of scientific historical probability. For example, many argue that the picture of Jesus eating with sinners and tax-collectors and other dubious characters escapes the net and can therefore be taken as established. Again, Jesus' proclamation of the kingdom of God as about to come with all the blessings of salvation, is held to be characteristic neither of the early church nor of contemporary Judaism, and also therefore established. Even if we start from a strictly sceptical position, and not from faith at all, there is a good deal of important material that cannot be doubted by any reasonable person, or so it is argued.

Other scholars, including many British ones, and among German scholars notably Joachim Jeremias, in effect approach the question from the other end. Instead of assuming material to be inauthentic unless it escapes the critical net, they assume it to be authentic unless proved otherwise. Obviously much more material will escape this much more wide-meshed net. What both approaches have in common is that they find it worthwhile to try to prove, as far as historical study ever can, that there is solid rock under the feet of faith. It does matter that the 'faith-image' (to borrow an expression from Norman Perrin) should be supported rather than contradicted by historical knowledge of Jesus.

Notes on Books

On the three kinds of answer
> H. K. McArthur, 'From the Historical Jesus to Christology', *Interpretation* 23(2,1969), pp. 190–206

Answer 1
> M. Green, *The Truth of God Incarnate*, Hodder & Stoughton, 1977, ch. 6

Answer 2
R. Bultmann, *Jesus Christ and Mythology*, SCM Press, 1958 – a good starter

R. Bultmann, *Jesus and the Word*, Collins/Fontana, 1958

H. W. Bartsch (ed.), *Kerygma and Myth*, SPCK, 1972 – fuller discussion

N. J. Young, *History and Existential Theology*, Epworth Press, 1969 – the most lucid introduction

Answer 3
G. Bornkamm, *Jesus of Nazareth*, Hodder & Stoughton, 1960 (pb 1973)

E. Käsemann, *Essays on New Testament Themes*, SCM Press, 1964, pp. 15–47

N. Perrin, *Rediscovering the Teaching of Jesus*, SCM Press, 1967

J. M. Robinson, *A New Quest of the Historical Jesus*, SCM Press, 1959

G. Aulén, *Jesus in Contemporary Historical Research*, SPCK, 1976

J. A. T. Robinson, *Can We Trust the New Testament?*, A. R. Mowbray, 1977

E. Trocmé, *Jesus and His Contemporaries*, SCM Press, 1973

How much do we really know?
A. Schweitzer, *The Quest of the Historical Jesus*, A. & C. Black, 1910

R. S. Barbour, *Traditio-Historical Criticism of the Gospels*, SPCK, 1972

B. F. Meyer, *The Aims of Jesus*, SCM Press, 1979

Perrin and Trocmé as above

Criteria of Authenticity
O. Betz, *What Do We Know About Jesus?* SCM Press, 1968

D. Cupitt and P. Armstrong, *Who Was Jesus?* BBC Publications, 1977

J. Jeremias, *New Testament Theology*, Vol. I, SCM Press, 1971, ch. 1

C. H. Dodd, *The Founder of Christianity*, Collins/Fontana, 1973

D. E. Nineham, epilogue to *Myth*

M. D. Hooker, 'On Using the Wrong Tool', *Theology* 75 (1972), pp. 570–581

Barbour, Bornkamm, Perrin and Robinson as above

On many of the questions in this chapter see also

H. K. McArthur (ed.), *In Search of the Historical Jesus*, Scribners, New York, 1969, and SPCK, 1970 – an excellent anthology and source-book

I. H. Marshall, *I Believe in the Historical Jesus*, Hodder & Stoughton, 1977, especially pp. 101–106 – a conservative treatment that accepts risk

S. W. Sykes and J. P. Clayton (eds.), *Christ, Faith and History*, Cambridge University Press, 1972, especially chs. 8–10

2. Do we have the wrong Jesus?

Once we accept that historical enquiry is a proper way to approach the gospels, we run the risk of getting the wrong answer – wrong from the point of view of Christian orthodoxy. Historians and journalists may – and do – announce with some regularity that we have the wrong picture of Jesus, who was really a substantially different sort of figure. Moreover in the last twenty years or so we have had the 'Dead Sea Scrolls Christ' (it had all happened before, or, Christianity was a secondhand copy of the beliefs of the Dead Sea sect), but almost nobody now takes this seriously. We have also had the grotesque mushroom Christ of John Allegro (*The Sacred Mushroom and the Cross*) – the whole Jesus story results from a prolonged collective 'good trip' on hallucinogenic mushrooms – which perhaps nobody ever did take seriously. We shall sample two of the alternative Christs, one of which is a serious and not entirely unorthodox contender, and the other of which has the interest of spectacular novelty.

A Secret Gospel

In 1958 Morton Smith of New York discovered what is generally agreed to be a genuine letter by Clement of Alexandria (late 2nd century). He found it in the ancient desert monastery of Mar Saba, near Jerusalem. The letter attacks the Carpocratians, a partly Christian sect who believed that in the name of Christian liberty bodily appetites must be given entirely free rein. They were in the strict sense a libertine group, who claimed to be the true heirs of Jesus; according to their secret tradition and secret gospel (of Mark), he was himself a libertine figure. Smith's letter of Clement in arguing against them quotes from a 'secret Gospel of Mark' in order to show that it does not say what the Carpocratians allege it does. Clement's quotation is as follows,

Immediately after the section which begins *And they were on the road, going up to Jerusalem* and continues to *after three days he will rise* [Mark 10:32–4] there follows, as the text goes, 'And they come to Bethany, and there was a woman there whose brother had died. She came and prostrated herself before Jesus and says to him, "Son of David, pity me". The disciples rebuked her, and Jesus in anger set out with her for the garden where the tomb was. Immediately a loud voice was heard from the tomb, and Jesus approached and rolled the stone away from the entrance to the tomb. And going in immediately where the young man was he stretched out his hand and raised him up, taking him by the hand. The young man looked on him and loved him, and began to beseech him that he might be with him. They came out of the tomb and went into the young man's house, for he was rich. After six days Jesus laid a charge upon him, and when evening came the young man comes to him, with a linen robe thrown over his naked body; and he stayed with him that night, for Jesus was teaching him the mystery of the kingdom of God. When he departed thence, he returned to the other side of the Jordan.'
After this there follows *And James and John came forward to him* and all that section [Mark 10:35–45]. But as for 'naked to naked' and the other things about which you wrote, they are not to be found. After the words *And he comes to Jericho* [Mark 10:46a] it adds only, 'And there was the sister of the young man whom Jesus loved and his mother and Salome; and Jesus did not receive them.' But as for the many other things which you wrote, they are falsehoods both in appearance and in reality. Now the true interpretation, which is in accordance with the true philosophy ...

There, alas, it stops. Clement obviously thinks this 'secret Gospel' represents genuine and old tradition, but he was a notoriously credulous person when it came to accepting dubious and spurious writings.

A Magical Christ

In 1973 Morton Smith published two books, one highly technical (*Clement of Alexandria and a Secret Gospel of Mark*), and one aimed at a more general readership (*The Secret Gospel*). He has since (1978) published a treatment of Jesus as he sees him, *Jesus the Magician*. This picture of Jesus is based partly on Clement's letter, for Smith accepts Clement's estimate of the reliability of the extract. It is based partly on what he finds said about Jesus in writings hostile to him, and it claims support from the New Testament itself. First then, he interprets the nocturnal meeting in the fragment to mean that this was the young man's initiation into the magical, esoteric, and libertine circle of Jesus, an initiation which may have included sexual contact. Jesus, in short, was a magician who, like many other magicians, claimed to be a god, who performed many miraculous acts, including exorcisms of course, and who as a god considered himself to be above all law, all human restrictions of any kind. His followers were admitted to a mystical union with him by baptism, and were consequently also free from all rules and restrictions. They had his spirit (in magical, not Old Testament terms) which made them essentially inhabitants of the supernatural realm.

All this was obviously potentially explosive doctrine, and was for initiates only. As a cover, in teaching the generality of people, the sort of ethical and eschatological figure familiar to us from our gospels was presented. Later, the secret magical tradition was lost both by the Gentile church under Paul, and by the Jerusalem church under James, but presumably survived in groups like the Carpocratians. In any case, it had always been the initiated few who were freed from controls; for the majority, the law was still valid.

In his more recent *Jesus the Magician*, Morton Smith concentrates on showing that according to his opponents Jesus was primarily a magician rather than a prophet or teacher. Much in our gospels shows awareness of this, either in inadvertently reflecting it, or in attempting to rebut it. In other words, intentionally or through sheer ignorance, the gospels and the church tradition generally are a cover-up. The real Jesus was a libertine, magical figure.

Against a Magical Christ
Despite Smith's acknowledged and massive learning, almost no one seems to be convinced by his case.
 1. His secret gospel fragment is widely suspected of being a 2nd-century fabrication, composed of bits and pieces from our Mark and our John. Early Christianity in Alexandria is in any case known to have been eccentric.
 2. His reading of the fragment has come under heavy fire on the grounds that he has read into it, not out of it, the night of magical initiation.
 3. The latest book does show that there are in the gospels some parallels with magical practices and expressions, but whether magic is the key to unlock the main door to Jesus, is quite another matter. It is often questionable whether these are the crucial parallels. If one approaches Jesus from a study of the Rabbis, one can easily find a Rabbinic Jesus, if from the mystery religions, a cult-figure Christ, if from the Scrolls, a Qumran Christ, and if from magical texts, a magical Christ. Smith tries to see too much through one pair of spectacles. It is far more likely, for instance, that calling Jesus 'son of God' arose because he was called and commissioned and empowered by Yahweh, than that it meant he claimed like other magicians to be a god. We need to show discrimination.
 4. For the libertine Christ there is no evidence at all, outside the curious writings of off-beat 2nd-century sects. The fact that in our gospels Jesus is not a legalist, by no means implies that he was an antinomian and libertine. Even the extract in Clement's letter does not really support this.
 5. To the theory of a cover-up, we can make the same reply

that Irenaeus gave in the 2nd century: if there were a secret tradition, why did people like Peter not pass it on to the leaders of the churches in Rome and elsewhere? A cover-up theory is suspect if only because something so widespread could not be covered up for long – too many people would be in the know. Yet in fact the very people who ought to have known best, apparently did not know at all!

We cannot deny that there are magical traits in the gospels, nor that his enemies classed Jesus as a magician (see Mark 3:21–7). The way in which different New Testament writers deal with these matters differently has been acutely described by J. M. Hull, *Hellenistic Magic and the Synoptic Tradition* (1974). Smith unfortunately tends to see what suits his case, without adequately considering whether the total picture does not fit other models, e.g. the messianic, better than the magical one. If he had subjected his own case to the rigorous criticism he applies to the identification of Jesus as a prophet, it would not stand. Certainly, for example, Jesus sometimes taught his disciples privately, but he is also recorded as saying that what they heard secretly they were to proclaim upon the housetops (Matt. 10:27; Luke 12:3).

It must, I think, be conceded that if Smith's case were found to be watertight, then the Christianity of those whose faith goes beyond, but not against the evidence, would be in dire jeopardy.

The Zealots

The position is different for those who see Jesus as having been not a-political but an active sympathizer with the left-wing revolutionaries of his day. Adherence to this view need not imperil anything in traditional Christianity, except its passive acceptance of the political establishment. The Zealots were the Palestinian freedom-fighters of the first century. Palestine had been an occupied country for half a millennium, apart from a break of about a century. At the time of Jesus, Rome was the occupying power and was inevitably resented, feared, and hated. Equally inevitably, there was an active but

28

clandestine resistance movement. I say 'inevitably', not because at that time there was similar resistance everywhere in the Roman world, but because of the peculiar nature of Israel as a nation under God. Israel's view of herself was always essentially theocratic: Palestine was God's gift to her, to be held in trust, and men and women were linked together in community under God, the God of the covenant. Their laws demonstrate the impossibility of separating religious and secular, for all was religious, all obedience was part of the nation's response and responsibility to God – whether concerning how to make a sacrifice or how close to reap to the edge of a field. Ritual laws, moral laws, social and even ecological laws, rub shoulders (see for instance Deuteronomy 22–24), thus betraying that these distinctions are ours, not ancient Israel's. Life was one whole under God. This wholeness now was disrupted by foreign occupation, and resistance was both political and religious, the two scarcely to be distinguished.

Some who opposed the occupation did so passively, waiting for God to act. Others, who at least from 66 AD were known as 'Zealots', took to the hills and fought as guerrillas. Whether we can so name them as early as the time of Jesus, and whether they were tightly organized groups at this stage, are both uncertain. I shall use 'Zealot' as convenient shorthand, without implying that they had been such a tightly organized group continuously from the time of Judas the Galilean (6 AD), as some maintain. These Zealots in 66 AD raised a wholesale rebellion against the Romans, seized control of Jerusalem, and withstood a siege there for four years before being almost totally wiped out, Jerusalem and the temple with them. The remnants made a last stand at Herod's old fortress, Masada by the Dead Sea, ending with their mass suicide in 73 AD (or 74 AD, as some now think) the night before the Romans breached the defences. To the end, they expected Yahweh to come to their aid, for they saw themselves as much as Yahweh-fighters as freedom-fighters.

Especially because of their destruction of the Jerusalem city archives which removed evidence of debts owed by the poor to the rich, they have been acclaimed as the enemies of all exploitation, not just the foreign variety (see Josephus, *Jewish War*, II 426–7).

A Zealot Christ?

Particularly since the work of S. G. F. Brandon (*The Fall of Jerusalem and the Christian Church*, 1951, and *Jesus and the Zealots*, 1967), it has been argued by a few scholars, some popularizers, and some Christians anxious for social and political revolution, that Jesus was a Zealot-sympathizer. Moreover, it has been held that his earliest followers were pro-Zealot largely, that the early Jerusalem church was very much in favour of the revolution of 66 AD, but that it died with the fall of Jerusalem in 70. Meanwhile, under the influence of Paul, a different stream of Christianity had emerged, a stream which understandably played down the nationalist and political nature of Christ and of primitive Palestinian Christianity, because it wished to live at peace within the Roman Empire, and because it was largely composed of non-Jews. It was this alone which survived the holocaust of 70 in any strength, and was responsible for the New Testament. Consequently, the original nature of the movement was obscured for later generations, though with skilful scholarly detective work, such as that of Brandon, it may be recovered at least in outline.

The more traditional view has been that Jesus' messiahship was non-political, either because 'his kingdom was not of this world' or because to bring in the kingdom was strictly God's work, or both. All earthly political arrangements are merely provisional, and will shortly be abolished by God. Meanwhile, the important matters are spiritual, not political, and we must simply accept the existing powers (like Paul in Romans 13).

Obviously, left-wing Christians are likely to be excited by the possibility of an explicitly left-wing Christ, and right-wing Christians to find it virtually blasphemous. But what of the evidence?

Evidence for Jesus as a Zealot-Sympathizer
1. Jesus came proclaiming the message of the kingdom (Mark 1:15, and often). He came from Galilee, suspicious in itself, for Galilee was known as a hot-bed of revolution (cf. Acts 5:37; Luke 13:1–2). Arguably, his message that the kingdom of God was at hand (Mark 1:15; Matt. 10:7 etc.) could be understood by his contemporaries only to mean that the political kingdom under God was about to be restored to Israel (see Acts 1:6; Luke 24:21). Unlike us, who are the heirs of centuries of Christian spiritualizing interpretation, Jesus' first hearers would assume he meant literally what he said. God's direct rule was about to be re-asserted, and Jesus was the herald or even the agent of that re-assertion. In practical terms, the Romans would be thrown out of Palestine, though that was only the first step. It was natural that when, according to John 6:15, Jesus had fed the 5000 in the wilderness, the people took Jesus and tried to make him king.
2. Jesus was recognized as messiah. There was at this time a variety of conceptions of messiah, but the dominant one was the Davidic: the messiah would be another David, a successful political and probably military leader, under God. If Jesus did claim, explicitly or implicitly, to be the messiah, this would be taken to mean that he would lead a revolt that was bound to succeed. It is claimed that the triumphal entry and the cleansing of the temple are such a revolt. The temple-cleansing could not have been done without considerable force, and indeed it is appropriate to speak of the *occupation* of the temple, which was intended to inaugurate the new regime. In the first instance it was a blow at the priestly aristocracy who controlled the temple, but implicitly it was a blow at their masters, the Romans.
3. Jesus was crucified as a revolutionary. The rising failed, and Jesus was arrested. Though his followers did make armed resistance in the Garden of Gethsemane (Mark 14:47; Luke 22:36–8) such resistance was futile, for a whole Roman cohort (John 18:3) was sent against them. Jesus stood trial as a terrorist, and was executed as one; this is made quite clear

by the inscription over the cross, 'The King of the Jews' (Mark 15:26, and in all the other gospels too). The Romans could only have meant by this that he was crucified for being a rebel chief. Crucifixion in itself suggests this, for it was the punishment for rebellion.

4. Jesus was associated with Zealots, and was thus in sympathy with them and with their goals. At least one of his disciples was a Zealot, Simon the 'Cananaean' (Mark 3:18; Matt. 10:4), a term which uncharacteristically Mark does not translate, presumably because he wishes to conceal the fact that the church had its beginnings in revolt. Luke, at a safer distance from the disasters of the Jewish revolt and the fall of Jerusalem, reveals that Simon was a Zealot ('Zelotes', Luke 6:15). Quite possibly others were Zealots too – James and John, the 'Sons of Thunder' perhaps, and of course Judas Iscariot, whose name may be a corruption of *sicarius*, meaning 'assassin'. We cannot assume that Simon (or the others) stopped being a Zealot on becoming a disciple. Moreover, Jesus never attacks the Zealots. He was associated with them in policy: his disciples were to carry arms (Luke 22:35–8, cf. Matt. 10:34), and he was concerned about social injustice and political oppression (Luke 6:24; 12:16–21; 16:19–31; Mark 10:17–25; Luke 13:32; Mark 10:42ff).

5. This picture has been obscured in our gospels in the interests of self-preservation. The tragic events of 70 AD ending in the destruction of Jerusalem, led the surviving non-Zealot Christians elsewhere in the Empire to fear that they would be convicted as fellow-travellers of rebels. They had to go on living under Roman rule, and wished to be free from suspicion, and wrote the gospels in such a way as to show the political harmlessness of Christianity. Jesus had been executed as a rebel – that could not be denied – but he had been *unjustly* so executed and had in reality been neither a Zealot nor a Zealot-sympathizer. It was all the fault of the Jewish leadership which hoodwinked the Roman authorities into believing Jesus was a political threat. In fact he was a *religious* threat to the Jewish leaders themselves.

In support of this view is the widely conceded fact that our gospels do, in one way or another, tend to play down the Roman part in the death of Jesus, and stress the Jewish, but cannot obliterate the actuality that Jesus was crucified by the Romans as a revolutionary leader. This quasi-Zealot view of Jesus is not incompatible with a belief in his divinity and it does not threaten orthodox Christianity in the way that Smith's magical Jesus does. Its effect is more on Christian morality than on belief, for if correct, it tends to support Christian participation in the revolutions and freedom struggles of our own time. It is difficult to look at this theory objectively; the way we react to it has probably a good deal to do with our own political stance. We must therefore take care not to import modern political debates in the first century, and not to decide an historical issue by contemporary political preferences. In other words, we must weigh the evidence.

The Case against a Zealot-type Christ
Brandon's case in favour is governed by a massive assumption, that those gospel passages which seem to show Jesus a Zealot-sympathizer are genuine, and reflect the true situation, but that those which point in the other direction are the work of the early church and of the evangelists (the gospel-writers) in their perilous post-70 situation. This effectively predetermines the answer, and we cannot make such an assumption. Following the five points made above, we now consider what tells against that case.

1. Jesus' teaching about the kingdom, in line with apocalyptic teaching generally, is about what *God* will do. Apocalyptic is an unveiling of divine intentions, not of human possibilities, and in the case of Jesus, we have an announcement, not a programme. In so far as the kingdom was a contemporary idea, it was a varied one, but in the usage of Jesus it is consistently about the *divine* action (and did not even rule out political obedience, Mark 12:13–17; Matt. 17:24–27). Indeed his followers are not to be concerned with the usual power game at all (Mark 10:42–45; Luke 22:24–27). On the contrary, the watchword is not activism, but readiness, for

God is about to act, and may already be acting (Luke 17:20–21).

2. When Jesus is called messiah, this could imply a revolutionary political leader. This is indeed what it is most likely to have implied to the contemporaries of Jesus, but the messiahship of Jesus is curiously elusive. After his crucifixion and resurrection he was undoubtedly acclaimed as messiah, though as time went on the original meaning was forgotten by the church. But did he claim to be messiah? In what is still usually held to be the earliest gospel, Mark, there is a strange reticence about the matter, as there is in several places in Matthew and Luke as well. In Mark, Jesus never claims to be messiah, though others so address him. When on three occasions the matter is directly put to him, he gives odd and ambiguous answers, except, according to some manuscripts, before the High Priest (Mark 14:62). There have been many theories to explain this reticence, but the position is so unclear that we cannot argue from his messiahship to his having been a Zealot-type leader. There are even hints (e.g. Acts 2:36) that he became messiah only at the resurrection, and that the term at first referred more to his future than to his past role (Acts 3:20).

Further, the triumphal entry is to be understood, in terms of Zechariah 9:9, as a humble and lowly affair, not a military event. The cleansing of the temple was not an occupation, armed or otherwise, for if it had been the Roman garrison in Fortress Antonia overlooking the temple would have promptly acted, and there would have been bloodshed there and then. It is unlikely that Josephus could have overlooked any such event, for he purports to give a comprehensive account of Jewish reactions to Roman rule, but he never mentions it. The 'cleansing' must therefore have been a low-key, prophetic-symbolism type of action, which was not nationalistic (Mark 11:17) though it was indeed against exploitation.

3. Jesus was indeed crucified by the Romans as a rebel, but this was a miscarriage of justice because of Roman misapprehension. It is true that the trial accounts bristle with histor-

ical problems, and it is never made clear precisely why the Jewish authorities wished to be rid of Jesus, and it is still a matter of debate whether they themselves at this time had the power of capital punishment. If they did, why did they have to persuade the Romans to condemn and execute him? Brandon may be right that when Jesus attacked the collaborating priestly aristocracy's control of the temple, they in effect said, 'If you attack us, you attack our Roman patrons,' and that the quickest and most foolproof solution was to hand him over to the Romans as a rebel. The religious and the political questions were thus so intertwined that from the High Priests' point of view it was arguable that Jesus *was* a political threat. The title over the cross, 'the King of the Jews', thus represents the way in which the matter was presented to the Romans, who mistakenly accepted it. They would not have understood Jesus' proclamation of God's kingdom, but if they had they might still have found it objectionable and treasonable.

As for the sayings about swords, and the incident in Gethsemane where a sword is used, they remain problems. Yet 'not peace but a sword' is clearly intended metaphorically; conceivably the command to take arms had in mind not the Roman army, but wild beasts and brigands, as Martin Hengel has suggested; and certainly no real armed resistance was offered in the Garden of Gethsemane (compare Luke 22:50 with Mark 14:47, and the following verses in both passages).

4. The association of Jesus with Zealots is less certain than it seems, for it is disputed whether 'Zelotes' in Luke 6:15 or Mark's 'Cananaean' were technical terms at the time. They may have simply meant something like 'enthusiast'. Indeed Luke's use of the term in Acts does not support the view that it was a technical term for him. More to the point are the strongly anti-Zealot indications: Jesus associates with the hated, collaborating tax-collectors (see Mark 2:14–17; Luke 15, and often), and to the Zealots this would be betrayal; on occasion Jesus shows marked friendliness to Roman officials (Matt. 8:5–13; Luke 7:1–10). His rejection of over-strict legalism would be as offensive to the Zealots as to the Pharisees. His talk about loving enemies (e.g. Matt. 5:44)

35

and his teaching against violence (Matt. 5:39; Luke 6:29) would have puzzled a Zealot, as would his attitude to Gentiles (e.g. Matt. 8:10–12; Luke 13:28–9) and even to Samaritans, for he tells a story about a *good* Samaritan (Luke 10). No self-respecting group of Zealots would tolerate someone like this.

Finally, even if there was at least one Zealot in the twelve, there was also one tax-collector!

5. A cover-up operation in the early church, resulting in a misleading picture of Jesus cannot be ruled out as impossible from the start. Just conceivably everything that tells against a Zealot-sympathizing Jesus could be there because the church is trying to save its skin and safeguard its position in the Roman world. Yet the evidence of Paul tells decisively against such a supposition. When he wrote, the Jerusalem church was, according to Brandon, strongly in sympathy with the rising tide of Zealotism. Now we know that Paul was in some controversy with that church over matters connected with the Law, but no hint of this other matter can be detected. Paul indeed is forever defending his gospel, or his version of the gospel, against legalism, probably against an early form of Gnosticism, against extreme asceticism, and against extreme libertinism – but he never defends it against revolutionary nationalism. If Brandon's picture is correct, this is incredible. In Romans 13 he talks about Christians and the state, but neither there nor elsewhere is there any indication that Christians were under any Jewish Christian pressure to be revolutionaries, nor under any Roman suspicion of the same thing. This highly important circumstance makes the whole Zealot-Christ picture unlikely in the extreme.

If original Christianity was firmly nationalistic and narrowly political, it is inexplicable that Paul or anyone else should think it a good prospect as a universal religion. Moreover, the Romans, once Jesus was killed, did not pursue his followers as being politically dangerous. It was not until the time of Nero that there was any state persecution of Christians, and that was far from the land and problems of Palestine.

Conclusion

The Zealot-sympathizing Christ never existed. It must be said that Brandon himself was much more cautious than some, such as Joel Carmichael, who have used his findings, and was careful to point out that he never said that Jesus was a Zealot. In turn, we must be cautious in our rejection: to reject the Zealot-sympathizer does not oblige us to accept a figure who happily accepts the status quo. Jesus was not an anti-revolutionary any more than a revolutionary; he did not fit into our categories at all, nor did he share the modern view that power comes from the people who can and ought to rise up against any who prevent their exercise of that power. Nevertheless he was critical of the way power was exercised, and critical also of the possession of wealth. The kingdom he proclaimed was not a merely personal, interior matter, but was about community, and looked to a future realization of present beginnings. Like the Pharisees, he probably believed that change would come through God's intervention and not through political action.

In a sense, Jesus was more revolutionary than the revolutionaries. This has been brilliantly shown by Milan Machoveč in one of the best books ever written about Jesus by a non-Christian (he is a Czech Marxist philosopher): the aims of Jesus were more fundamental than those of the Zealots, not less, for he started with the inner man and embraced everything – and above all was concerned that the future, God's future, should totally control the present. We cannot give Jesus our dilemmas and choices, nor the issues of our century and our society. He continues to put questions against all our preoccupations and concerns, for not only does he fail to be confined by our categories, but perpetually makes us ask if we have the right ones.

Notes on Books

Introduction
> J. M. Allegro, *The Sacred Mushroom and the Cross*, Hodder & Stoughton, 1970

J. M. Allegro, *The Dead Sea Scrolls*, Penguin Books, 1956

A Secret Gospel

M. Smith, *Clement of Alexandria and a Secret Gospel of Mark*, Harvard University Press, Cambridge Mass., 1973

M. Smith, *The Secret Gospel,* Harper & Row, New York, 1973

A Magical Christ

M. Smith, *Jesus the Magician*, Gollancz, 1978

Against a Magical Christ

F. F. Bruce, *The 'Secret' Gospel of Mark*, Athlone Press, 1974

J. M. Hull, *Hellenistic Magic and the Synoptic Tradition*, SCM Press, 1974

The Zealots

W. R. Farmer, *Maccabees, Zealots, and Josephus*, Columbia University Press, New York, 1956

D. M. Rhoads, *Israel in Revolution 6–74 C.E.,* Fortress Press, Philadelphia, 1977 – based on Josephus

A Zealot Christ?

S. G. F. Brandon, *The Fall of Jerusalem and the Christian Church*, 3rd edn, SPCK, 1978

S. G. F. Brandon, *Jesus and the Zealots*, Manchester University Press, 1967

P. Winter, *On the Trial of Jesus*, W. de Gruyter, Berlin, 1961

J. Carmichael, *The Death of Jesus*, Gollancz, 1963 – an attempt to popularize the findings of Brandon and Winter, important mainly for the astonishing impact it had in Germany, thanks to discussion of it in *Der Spiegel*

Evidence for Jesus as Zealot Sympathizer

See previous section

The Case against a Zealot-type Christ

O. Cullmann, *Jesus and the Revolutionaries*, Harper & Row, New York, 1970

M. Hengel, *Was Jesus a Revolutionist?* Fortress Press, Philadelphia, 1971

M. Hengel, *Victory over Violence*, SPCK, 1975

E. Bammel (ed.), *The Trial of Jesus*, SCM Press, 1970 –
does not have a doctrinaire position, but is useful on the
historical problems
Conclusion
M. Machoveč, *A Marxist Looks at Jesus*, Darton, Longman
& Todd, 1976
H. J. Cadbury, *The Peril of Modernizing Jesus*, SPCK, 1962

3. Do we know what Jesus thought about himself?

Jesus proclaims the kingdom of God, but does not make explicit claims for himself. This is an oversimplification, but is largely true so far as Matthew, Mark, and Luke, the 'Synoptic' gospels, are concerned. It is not true at all of John's gospel, where Jesus talks very little about the kingdom of God, and a great deal about himself. It might be expected, therefore, that this chapter would be mainly about John's gospel; in fact I shall scarcely mention it. This is because for a long time the consensus of scholarship has taken it for granted that John is a highly interpreted version of the life and ministry of Jesus, a thoroughly 'theologized' picture (hence the title of a recent book on John, by S. S. Smalley, *John: Evangelist and Interpreter*, 1978). Everything is seen in the light of the outcome of the story, and Jesus is a glorious, heavenly, though persistently subordinate, figure from the beginning. Even the way in which Jesus speaks is quite different from his voice in the other gospels: his vocabulary, style, even the sorts of things he says, are all different. All the gospels see Jesus through the eyes of a community or an individual or both, but this is most obvious in the case of John, and to a much greater extent. Moreover, it seems likely that the Synoptics are from communities that have more in common with one another than any has with the community behind John's gospel, and that relationship to the Jewish community is one of the differentiating factors.

This is not to deny that there may be good history in John, however strongly tinted the theological spectacles, but it does mean that John's picture of Jesus belongs in a chapter by itself.

Does the Question Matter?

We have no direct access to what Jesus thought about anything. All we have is at second hand, and therefore to place too much reliance on discovering what Jesus thought about himself is to build on precarious foundations. The gospel writers were presumably not concerned to give us the inner thoughts of Jesus (how would they know them?) but to let his words and actions make their own impact on the reader. Their primary aim was not to satisfy the desire for a life-story, a biography in the modern sense. We have already seen how difficult it is to know whether or not he claimed to be messiah, yet we know that after the resurrection his followers acclaimed him as messiah. Why? If during his ministry neither his words nor his actions had prompted the thought, why should they want to give him that particular title? Nevertheless, supposing it could be proved that it never crossed Jesus' mind that he might be messiah, that would not debar his followers from recognizing him as such. It would be different if he had evidently and categorically denied being messiah. The point is that what he thought about himself, if we could discover it, would not necessarily determine what his followers could legitimately think about him, though it would place limitations. They could reasonably go *beyond* what he believed about himself, but not so reasonably *against* it. Therefore, we cannot avoid an interest in the question, but cannot allow it to be decisive.

Some theologians, committed to the view that Jesus must have had perfect knowledge of all that concerned his relationship with God, give his self-knowledge a more crucial role. This whole question we shall discuss later; all that I wish now to maintain is that from a vantage point after the resurrection, the church may conceivably see Jesus in a sharper light than even he did himself. The difficulties involved in the general question of how he saw himself are well illustrated by the strange case of 'the Son of man', which shows the real difficulties scholars have with the material. There are problems of meaning and problems of history.

The Figure of the Son of Man

In all four gospels, this is the one 'title' Jesus applies to himself, and one title that is exclusively on his lips; with the only apparent exception of John 12:34, other people do not use this term of him. Apart from Acts 7:56, it is peculiar to the gospels, nor does it occur in other early Christian writings, though much later it becomes a designation for the humanity of Jesus. It occurs over 60 times in the gospels. Surely then this must be the answer to what Jesus thought about himself? He thought he was Son of man (whatever that means – nowhere in the New Testament is it queried or explained). *Is* it some sort of title? Literally 'the son of the man', it was an Aramaic expression which when rendered into Greek was as incomprehensible as it is in English; perhaps its very mysteriousness led to its being regarded (erroneously) as some sort of title?

We may begin with the Old Testament, and with the book of Ezekiel, in which the prophet is very frequently addressed as '*a* son of man', i.e. without the articles, in Hebrew. Ezekiel does not refer to himself in this way. It occurs again without articles in Psalm 8:4, where it is a near synonym for 'man', perhaps meaning 'any particular man' (compare the two halves of the verse, and see also Psalm 80:17). The most frequently discussed Old Testament instance however is Daniel 7:13. Here, 'one like a son of man' is clearly meant to represent Israel, the truly human people, at present being oppressed by other, beastly, powers (compare 7:13 with 7:18, 22, 27). Thus in Daniel 7 as it stands, the term is not a title but a cryptic reference to Israel. None the less it is often argued that Daniel 7 and 'son of man' came to be understood in later times as referring to a heavenly redeemer who would descend at the End and redeem Israel from all bondage – a sort of supernatural and universal counterpart to the earthly, political, nationalist messiah. It is argued that this figure reappears in the late Jewish book of Enoch, chapters 37–71, the so-called 'Similitudes of Enoch', in the Ethiopian version. The figure, though not the 'title', is also held to be evident in 2

Esdras 13, in the Old Testament Apocrypha. Bearing all this in mind, many scholars have believed that at the time of Jesus there was the expectation of a glorious heavenly Son of man, and that in the New Testament Jesus is identified with this figure. The really strong piece of evidence for this identification is Mark 14:62 (and parallels in Matthew and Luke) where we find a slightly adapted quotation of Daniel 7:13,

> You will see the Son of man sitting at the right hand of power, and coming with the clouds of heaven (see also Mark 13:26 and parallels).

Is this a later development, a linking of Jesus with the Daniel figure when it was no longer remembered that 'Son of man' was not meant to be a title? Or is it the key to the whole thing? If the second, did Jesus make the identification, or did the church do it later, and how can we tell?

The position is undeniably complicated, and there are almost as many theories as there are scholars. Some have given the whole matter up as beyond solution. Rather than attempting the highly technical task of sifting the evidence and assessing the theories, I propose to set up somewhat arbitrarily three competing possibilities in general outline. In one form or another they are or have been held by important groups of scholars.

First View – A Self-Designation with New Content
Jesus, wary about being called 'messiah' because of its political overtones, preferred the enigmatic 'Son of man' simply because he could fill it with his own meaning. This meaning was very largely that of the Suffering Servant (Isaiah 53 in particular), thus re-interpreting the original and rather vague supernatural redeemer meaning. He is a heavenly figure (cf. Daniel 7:13, 2 Esdras, and the Similitudes of Enoch), but of a suffering kind. The term was thus pliant to his wishes, as the more fixed and narrowly nationalist 'messiah' was not. Exponents of this view used to be numerous, and for a long time it was critical orthodoxy in British scholarship. A passage like

Mark 8:29–31 was used to show that when charged with being messiah, Jesus said neither 'Yes' nor 'No', but switched the conversation to different terminology, namely 'Son of man', which he then explicitly filled with suffering connotations. Jesus, it was frequently said, fused the figures of Son of man and Suffering Servant.

Few now hold this view, which has been attacked at too many points to survive. The evidence for it never was very strong, but many people found it an illuminating hypothesis. We shall see that there are serious doubts about this heavenly, individual, Son of man redeemer figure; indeed, long ago T. W. Manson interpreted the term in *corporate* fashion in strict accord with the meaning in Daniel 7:13, to mean not just Jesus but Jesus in and with his community, the new Israel. A further blow hit the accepted synthesis when it was shown, notably for the English-speaking world by M. D. Hooker in *Jesus and the Servant*, 1959, that the evidence that Jesus consciously saw his mission in terms of the Suffering Servant's vicarious work was so scanty as to be effectively non-existent.

Second View — Jesus expected someone else as heavenly Son of Man

This view, particularly associated with Rudolf Bultmann, still exercises considerable influence in Germany. Like the first, it starts from the position that the term is a title which owed its currency to Daniel 7:13, but is interpreted in later Jewish thought, i.e. Enoch and 2 Esdras, so as to refer to an individual, heavenly redeemer. Jesus did *not* identify himself with this figure; Mark 8:38 and Luke 12:8f are evidence that he expected another in that role, who would vindicate him,

> And I tell you, everyone who acknowledges me before men, the Son of man also will acknowledge him before the angels of God (Luke 12:8).

After the resurrection, the early church took the step of identifying this coming figure with Jesus himself, though the original distinction between them can still be detected in passages like Luke 12:8.The identification made, the church began to think of Jesus as having always been the Son of man, and inserted the term into sayings from which it had been absent, sayings about his earthly situation (e.g. Matt. 8:20/Luke 9:58), and sayings about future suffering and vindication (e.g. Mark 8:31/Luke 9:22). This process of insertion can sometimes be detected as when in one gospel we have 'I' and in another 'the Son of man' in the same saying, e.g. Mark 8:27 compared with Matthew 16:13.

There is an assumption behind this view, in addition to the assumption that 'the Son of man' is the title of a glorious supernatural figure: it is that no sane good man could conceivably believe himself to be or claim to be any such thing. Anyone making such a claim would be mad, or a trickster, if the claim were false, or not a human being at all, if the claim were true. This assumption, usually tacit, has been made explicit by John Knox (in *The Death of Christ*, pp. 58–73). Jesus, says Knox, quite clearly was neither mad nor bad, and equally clearly was a human being. Therefore he did not claim to be Son of man, though this does not prevent our acknowledging that in God's intention this is what he was. Of course this raises the knotty question of what is and what is not compatible with true humanness, but we must note that even on this theory, the Son of man is not God; nevertheless he is supernatural and pre-existent, and it is reasonable to argue that anyone who thought of himself in such terms was hardly human on any usual definition.

There are serious difficulties with the whole theory, which has been losing its following quite drastically in the last few years. For one thing, it is debatable whether Mark 8:38 and Luke 12:8f really do distinguish between the Son of man and Jesus. Secondly, the theory makes Jesus a forerunner (who also *has* a forerunner, John the Baptist) rather than a fulfilment figure, and this goes against so much in the New Testament that it demands a good deal of swallowing. Thirdly, there is no obvious reason why the resurrection should make the church identify Jesus with the Son of man – they might equally well have taken it that here was divine endorsement of the certainty that the Son of man would come. Perhaps above all, if it was the community that made the identification, why did they put the title only on the lips of Jesus, and *never* on those of the disciples, i.e. the church, and why should the community do this when there is virtually no evidence that they were interested in or understood the term? It is interesting that 'the Son of man' would survive the criterion of dissimilarity, because it was neither an early church concern nor a common Jewish conception. Finally, what has accelerated the loss of confidence in this theory is the suspicion that 'the Son of man' never was a title.

Third View – Not a Title for a Glorious Supernatural Figure
This is harder to pinpoint because it is more an agreed approach than a concrete position. Increasing doubt has been cast on the whole notion of a supernatural, redeeming Son of man in contemporary Judaism. Doubt is also cast on whether it is *any* sort of title. Some, though not all, Semitists are now arguing that it was a quite possible if not usual way of referring to oneself in a deprecating way: it simply means 'I'. Nevertheless, it is found in quotation of Daniel 7:13, so at some stage a link was made with the Danielic figure. Even here, however, it is doubted whether any more is meant than that Son of man (i.e. Israel) represents true humanity, as against the beasts (i.e. kingdoms of the oppressors) which represent inhumanity. The oppressed humanity will eventually be vindicated and delivered by God. If 'the Son of man' in the gospels means any more than 'I', it refers to the oppressed, humiliated one (or ones) who will be vindicated and delivered by God. As for the Similitudes of Enoch, and 2 Esdras, both are post-Christian and irrelevant. Even if the Similitudes are dated early enough to be relevant, it can be argued that they deal with the term in the same way as Daniel 7. There is no trace of the 'title' anywhere else.

Some say that the connection with Daniel 7:13 was made by the church and not by Jesus, after the transition from Aramaic to Greek, and therefore when the original meaning of the term had been forgotten. On the other hand it is

46

possible that Jesus, accustomed to refer to himself self-deprecatingly as the Son of man, came to see himself also as oppressed but destined to be vindicated, in terms of Daniel 7. C. F. D. Moule argues that the virtually invariable presence of the article, *the* Son of man, suggests that a specific model is in mind, the likeliest being Daniel 7:13, and so a humiliated figure who looks to God for vindication both for himself and for the community he represents. At any rate, whether by Jesus or by the early church, the move was made from simple self-reference to a Daniel 7 interpretation. The move is not a difficult one, for Daniel 7 is taken to be *not* about a glorious heavenly redeemer.

Some think that the equivalence of the term with 'man' is important, and that if Jesus is saying anything at all in using it, he is refusing to be put into people's ready-made categories. He is claiming to come not just as a Jew, especially a Zealot-type Jew, but as a human being whose mission is to human beings, whether Jews or Samaritans, Romans or tax-collectors, prostitutes or lepers. Perhaps in Galatians 3:28 Paul has picked up this intention of Jesus. It is possible, but we are engulfed in uncertainties. We do not know for sure what the term meant; we do not know for sure whether it began as a designation for another, future figure; we do not know for sure whether or not Jesus used the term of himself. For what it is worth, my own view is that it was not an early church expression, and that some form of the third view is probably correct.

Implicit Christology

Our excursion into the meaning of 'the Son of man' has not been encouraging; New Testament scholarship has been notably unsuccessful in solving the problem. Can we then know anything of Jesus' view of himself? In fact we can. Occasionally Jesus refers to himself as a prophet (Mark 6:4/Matt. 13:57; Luke 13:33), and more frequently other people acclaim him as one, though the early church found it an inadequate way of describing him. It may therefore be an ancient view which Jesus himself shared. More fruitful is an examination of his role as proclaimer of the kingdom, for he clearly saw himself as having a key function in it and not just as a herald. One of the prominent features of his proclamation is that the kingdom is imminent (Mark 1:15 etc.), but another is that in his own words and actions the kingdom is already at work. This is seen in his healings, his exorcisms, and his call to decision. In his ministry the kingdom of God opposes the kingdom of evil (e.g. Luke 11:20/Matt. 12:28), and perhaps most notably of all, his consorting with tax-collectors and other bad characters is held up as the model of how *God* treats men and women (see for example Luke 15; Matt. 20:1–16). Indeed this is the point of his behaving as he does, and we have already seen that this consorting with the unacceptable is one of the firmest historical elements in the Jesus tradition. Its importance is thus very considerable.

Some, especially Joachim Jeremias, believe that Jesus' use of 'Abba' in addressing God (untranslated in Mark 14:36, and presumably lying behind 'Father' elsewhere in the gospels) was unprecedented. It may not in fact be quite unprecedented, but it was highly unusual, and may indicate that Jesus felt himself to be in a peculiar intimacy with God, for 'Abba' is the family, not the liturgical word. Again, the fact that Jesus habitually says not 'Thus saith the Lord', but simply 'But *I* say unto you' as in Matthew 5, and elsewhere commonly 'Amen I say to you', may also indicate an implicit claim for unusual personal authority. The intimacy and the authority may belong together, and both are widely agreed to be of high historical probability.

All these things may be pointers to Jesus' own sense of his specialness. On the other hand an implicit christology must also take account of the gospel emphasis on the humanness of Jesus: his dependence on God, his vocation from God, his prayer to God, his sense of distance from God as in Mark 15:34, even his sense of sonship, all imply a clear distinction between Jesus and God. A simple reversible equation, Jesus equals God, has rightly never been a tenet of orthodox Christian belief.

Conclusion

For those who want to find a divine Jesus, we may not seem to have got very far. Intimacy with God and great authority from him are not the same thing as being – or believing oneself to be! – divine. It is important, of course, not to read the Nicene Creed into the gospels, for it is an interpretation of them, and not *vice versa*. On the other hand, we must not adopt an interpretation of the gospels and of Jesus himself, which makes the development of belief in him totally incomprehensible. There must have been something in what he was, and in what happened, to make it reasonable for his followers in less than a generation to think of him as God's vice-gerent, and then as in some sense God. So far, we have found an examination of 'titles', like Son of man and messiah, disappointingly unhelpful. Oddly enough, it is when we move on to 'implicit christology', i.e. start reading between the lines, as we have just been doing, that we begin to find indications that Jesus did see himself as a significant figure in the dealings of God with the human race.

Notes on Books

Introduction

S. S. Smalley, *John: Evangelist and Interpreter*, Paternoster Press, 1978

J. Painter, *John: Witness and Theologian*, SPCK, 1975 – another useful account of the nature of John's gospel

The Figure of the Son of Man

J. D. G. Dunn, *Unity and Diversity in the New Testament*, SCM Press, 1977, pp. 35–40

I. H. Marshall, *The Origins of New Testament Christology*, Inter-Varsity Press, 1977, ch. 4

E. Schweizer, *Jesus*, SCM Press, 1971, pp. 18–21, 54–59

First View

M. D. Hooker, *Jesus and the Servant*, SPCK, 1959 – against

A. M. Hunter, *The Work and Words of Jesus*, SCM Press, 1950, pp. 84–87 – for

A. Richardson, *An Introduction to the Theology of the New*

Testament, SCM Press, 1958, ch. 6 – for
E. Stauffer, *New Testament Theology*, SCM Press, 1955, ch. 24 – for
T. W. Manson, *The Teaching of Jesus*, Cambridge University Press, 1931, pp. 211–233 – corporate view
Second View
R. Bultmann, *Theology of the New Testament*, Vol. I, SCM Press, 1952, pp. 26–32
F. Hahn, *The Titles of Jesus in Christology*, Lutterworth Press, 1969, ch. 1
J. Knox, *The Death of Christ*, Collins, 1959, pp. 58–73
Third View
M. D. Hooker, *The Son of Man in Mark*, SPCK, 1967
C. F. D. Moule, *The Origin of Christology*, Cambridge University Press, 1977, pp. 11–22
G. Vermes, *Jesus the Jew*, Collins, 1973, ch. 7
See also the articles by M. Black and G. Vermes in the first number of *Journal for the Study of the New Testament*, October 1978
Implicit Christology
J. D. G. Dunn, *Jesus and the Spirit*, SCM Press, 1975, pp. 21–40
J. Jeremias, *New Testament Theology*, Vol. I, SCM Press, 1971, ch. 1
N. Perrin, *The Kingdom of God in the Teaching of Jesus*, SCM Press, 1963
N. Perrin, *Rediscovering the Teaching of Jesus*, SCM Press, 1967, ch. 3

II

The Question of what the New Testament says

4. Was there an Evolution of Christology in the New Testament?

Jesus made a striking impression on those who met him, whether they responded to him and became disciples, or rejected him. They thought of him as a Rabbi (teacher), a prophet, perhaps as messiah, or perhaps as a clever magician – but none of these responses goes beyond human description. Yet within less than one generation he was being described in superhuman terms, and within at the most three generations he was described as one with the Father, God's eternal Word (John 17:11; 1:1,14). Thus in Philippians 2:9–11 Paul, probably quoting earlier tradition in the form of a hymn, can give to Christ a place and a rank almost equal to God himself, and in 1 Corinthians 8:6 talk of Christ as the one through whom all things exist, the Lord of the universe, no less. This cosmic lordship is even more strongly stressed in the later letters to the Colossians and to the Ephesians, where Christ is the agent of creation as he is of redemption. We are so familiar with all this that we tend not to notice how extra-ordinary it is. Somehow, within a generation, a human being is taken to be the agent of creation, God's vice-gerent (if not more). How did this come about? Was it all implicit from the beginning, or was there a massive change at some point.?

The question gets different answers. Some scholars have long held that as the church moved out of a purely Palestinian and Jewish setting, the Jewish messiah-figure, who was God's agent but in himself a strictly human figure, becomes transmuted into a heavenly divine redeemer. This happened in Christian circles under Hellenistic influence, where there was not too sharp a distinction made between divine and human, quite unlike Jewish circles where the distinction was never compromised. Others, and most recently C. F. D. Moule in *The Origin of Christology* (1977), agree that there was development, but along a line already set, so that there was no basic shift, no fundamental turnabout or evolution.

Jewish Beginnings

Jesus and his first followers were all Jews, and Jews who were anything like orthodox never lost sight of the oneness of God. 'The Lord our God is one . . .' Like Muslims, they were and are famous for undeviating monotheism. Indeed God acted in the world, and would act in the future, to redress the palpable wrongs, injustices, and oppression under which the Jews themselves were notable sufferers. Whether the agents of this action were human or angelic, there was never any doubt that they were subordinate to God and less than divine. God was without rival, without parts, and without division. Jews could therefore easily see Jesus as God's agent, God's very special agent perhaps, and they could also see God, through his Spirit, as present in Jesus to a remarkable degree (e.g. 2 Cor. 5:19). What they could not do without infringing on the rights of the one God, Yahweh, was to see Jesus as God. It is not surprising that the small Jewish Christian groups of later centuries were noted for not regarding Jesus as divine. Seeing him as messiah, Son of man, even Lord, could be reconciled with their monotheism but equating him with God was a step as obnoxious to them as it is to Jews today.

Hellenistic Developments

As the first century wore on, the church became progressively less Jewish and more Gentile in composition, and for practical purposes, Gentile meant (Hellenistic) Greek. Hellenism is the name given to that development of Greek culture and thought which followed in the wake of the conquests of Alexander the Great, a development which worked two ways. On the one hand, the victorious Greeks through their colonies spread Greek ideas everywhere, but on the other hand they were in turn affected by the indigenous cultures, ways of thought, religions and customs which they had set out to replace. Because of this two-way process, the Hellenism of our period is a different phenomenon from the Greek culture of the classical age. Greece imposed her culture on the east, but over the centuries the east retaliated, so that Hellenism is a hybrid, syncretistic affair. Persia in particular had a strong counter-influence. Obviously, then, there was no single Hellenistic way of thinking about God, yet there were crucial differences from the Jewish outlook, and these certainly made it easier to speak of Jesus as God.

1. Although there was the idea of one supreme God, it was relatively easy to think of gods in the plural. In some strands of thought divinity was a spiritual substance, a very fine substance, which could be shared among a number of beings, and of which there could be more or less. According to some views, there was divinity in all people, and in any case the distance between men and God (or gods) was not an infinite one but a matter of degree. It was thus possible to think of a being that was partly divine and partly human. A 'Son of God' was not a difficult conception – it meant someone with an unusually large element of divinity which became evident through his miraculous powers, for instance. Human beings were made up of earthly body, and soul (or mind, or spirit) which is at least sometimes taken to be akin to the divine. This whole understanding of man made it easier to think of divine persons who were also human, like Jesus Christ.

2. There were religions, cults, which aimed at giving a person experience of a god, or a god-like figure, through esoteric rituals which led to the identification of the initiate with the god of the cult. These gods or 'lords' were important not so much for their divine status as for their ability to secure eternal life and deliverance from fate for their devotees. Whether or not these 'gods many and lords many' (1 Cor. 8:6) had ever historically existed, hardly mattered. What did matter was the devotees' experience of fellowship with one another and with the lord, and their consequent liberation and immortality.

3. It is likely that what later came to be called *Gnosticism*

was already active in the first century. If the later Gnostic idea of a heavenly redeemer who descends to reassemble the dispersed particles of divinity, which have been scattered and imprisoned in human bodies, is to be inferred as early as this, then some hearers of the Christian message would perhaps understand Jesus as such a figure, a divine visitor from the realm of pure spirit into this crass earthly prison camp. It is now widely held, however, that this figure did not exert influence until the second century.

4. The lordship of the Roman Emperor, itself derived from oriental rather than Roman thinking about political power, was already being proclaimed in the eastern parts of the Empire. 'Caesar is lord' may already have been understood in a divine sense, though this acknowledgement was not required, even of Roman citizens, until the end of the century.

Out of all this, it is understandable that Jesus should be seen as a divine figure who – rather to the surprise of the syncretistic and tolerant spirit of the time – demanded exclusive attachment. 'Christ' would be a puzzling title, and rapidly became simply part of his name. 'Son of God', 'lord', or even 'god', were more comprehensible. It was a completely Hellenized church that formulated such sophisticated statements as the Nicene Creed and the Definition of Chalcedon, yet there was on all this Hellenism a constant brake. The church did move from a Jewish to a Greek setting, but she never abandoned her Jewish, monotheistic roots. Jesus could therefore never be a second god alongside Yahweh; that simple solution was forever forbidden.

The move was not made abruptly from one setting to the other, for more or less in the middle we find the phenomenon of Hellenistic Judaism.

Hellenistic Judaism

By the time of Jesus, Judaism itself had been to varying degrees penetrated by the Hellenistic spirit and by Hellenistic ways of thinking. This is most sharply evident in a writer like Philo, whose massive works produced in Alexandria in the first century AD are in large part an attempt to marry traditional Jewish religion with Greek philosophy. Recent studies, especially Martin Hengel's *Judaism and Hellenism*, have shown that even within Palestinian Judaism there had been extensive penetration by Hellenism – not less effective for being sometimes unrecognized. Within the early Jerusalem church too there were Hellenistic elements, as Acts 7 notes. Outside Palestine, the first converts were usually Jews, at least some of whom were doubtless Hellenized, living as they did in a Greek environment. It is noteworthy that when Paul quotes the Old Testament he almost invariably quotes from the Septuagint, the Greek translation, and does not make his own translation from the Hebrew (we can tell this because the Greek and Hebrew versions do not precisely correspond).

From a very early stage, therefore, perhaps from the very beginning, Christianity was embraced by people whose mental furniture was partly provided by Hellenism. This bears on their understanding of Jesus. Hellenistic Judaism was no less monotheistic than traditional Palestinian Judaism, but it was fruitful soil for a particular way of speaking about God's activity, through personified abstractions, and especially through the figure of *wisdom*. Rather than have God act directly, it sees wisdom (in Philo, the *Logos*, word, as well) as not just an attribute of God, but almost as a secondary power, an agent used by God. This is found in the book of Proverbs, but later Hellenistic Judaism developed the use until at times it is unclear whether metaphor remains metaphor, or has turned into reality.

Hellenistic Judaism also provides a setting in which interest can shift from the *function* of Jesus, to his *status*, his nature, and above all to a definition of his position in relation to God. On the other hand it provides a setting in which interest in Jesus as a Jewish messiah can diminish, and make way for the much more ethical and cosmological concerns which Hellenistic Judaism brought to nascent Christianity. The question of Jesus in relation to Israel never disappeared, but it did become less important than that of his relation to mankind.

The Issue of Development or Fundamental Change

In moving from a Palestinian Jewish setting through Hellenistic Judaism to its final home in Gentile Hellenism, did belief in Jesus remain essentially the same, simply adapting to different sets of conceptual tools, or was it fundamentally changed? Is the proclamation of Jesus as the divine Son, the Lord, the Logos, the same as or different from the recognition of him as messiah? There is serious cause to wonder if the problem is soluble, for reasons like the following.

1. Despite F. Hahn and R. H. Fuller, we cannot accept anything like three distinct phases. M. Hengel has shown that Palestinian and Hellenistic Judaism are not to be sharply differentiated: within and outside Palestine, the boundaries were fluid and ran through places, periods, writings, and individuals. They were so fluid that it is questionable whether we can work with them at all. Jews in Alexandria could be as nationalist and conservative as any in Palestine, and the most conservative Jew in Jerusalem could think in a thoroughly Hellenistic way. We cannot use these distinctions to map the development of christology, or not without great caution.

2. It is exceedingly difficult to know if something said in one set of terms (Jewish) means the same as something said in another set (Hellenistic). How far does the language and set of conceptions in which we express something, affect what we say? How can we tell if what the Jewish Christians meant by 'messiah' amounts to much the same as what Greek Christians meant by 'lord'? We have already said that Jews are commonly held to have thought about Jesus in terms of what he *did*, and Greeks in terms of what he *was*; do these finally amount to the same thing, or not? The question is illustrated by R. H. Fuller's *Foundations of New Testament Christology* (1965), in which he shows at length how in moving from one setting to another to another, the church's beliefs about Christ came to be expressed in terms and patterns appropriate to the successive settings. The impression easily gained is that he is talking about substantial changes in belief, yet towards the end of the book it emerges

that he does not think any fundamental change to have occurred. Despite the move from functional (Jewish) to ontological or 'nature' christology (Hellenistic), and despite a sharp distinction between parts of the material that belong to the different phases, Fuller states (pp. 254f) that what finally emerges was implicit all along.

3. The problem of chronology is acute. Later estimates of Jesus are not always or necessarily higher (i.e. more divine) than earlier ones. Paul's writings are the earliest in the New Testament, yet he includes some of the 'highest' christology, e.g. 1 Corinthians 8:6, Philippians 2:6–11; whereas Luke's writings are generally held to be late, yet his picture of Christ is far less lofty in comparison. Again, it simply cannot be assumed that Hellenistic elements are necessarily late ones, as 1 Corinthians 8:6 shows.

Rather than try to tackle the whole vast question, we shall limit ourselves once again to a specific example, that of the ascription of *kyrios* ('lord') to Jesus.

Jesus Christ is Lord

What does it mean when Jesus is addressed, or referred to, as lord? Does it make any difference who is speaking? Does it mean the same thing on the lips of a Jew and a Greek? Does it exhibit a development in meaning in line with what was there from the beginning, or radical change? We may begin by setting out what is known.

The Greek word *kyrios* can be used of any person, human or divine, who has authority. The vocative, *kyrie*, frequently found in the gospels, is nothing more than polite usage, equivalent to 'sir' in English. If someone calls me 'sir' it does not mean I have been knighted. So, in the gospels it is quite plain that some who politely call him *kyrie* have no belief in Jesus as lord, e.g. Matthew 8:2, 6, 8, and cf. Matthew 21:29, 30. These vocative instances may represent no more than ordinary courtesy and respect, and must be excluded from consideration.

Kyrios is a title of the Roman Emperor, and by the end of the first century AD a divine title, so that to call him *Kyrios*

Kaisar was to accept his divinity, which is why Christians could not call him that. The word could also be used of a divine being, e.g. the lord of a mystery cult, though here perhaps the main reference was not to his divine status but to his being master of the worshipper. Of course, one easily led to the other, cf. the 'gods many and lords many' of 1 Corinthians 8:6, though here they are probably associated rather than identified. *Kyrios* could also be used of a human master, as perhaps in Mark 11:3. The word thus has a spectrum of use, from the merely human to the divine, but probably always conveys the notion of legitimate as opposed to despotic authority. It is certainly correlative to *doulos*, 'servant'.

The early Christians' first confession was probably 'Jesus is Lord' (Rom. 10:9; 1 Cor. 12:3), at least in Greek-speaking circles. Earlier, in Palestine, did they use the roughly equivalent *mar* (Aramaic) and *adhon* (Hebrew) for Jesus? The answer usually given is that the original disciples certainly did not, for these would have associated *adhon* with Yahweh, and possibly *mar* too, and they could scarcely have wanted to say that Jesus was Yahweh. It must, therefore, have been in the Hellenistic church that Jesus was first called 'lord', or so the argument runs. Then as they read the Septuagint which used *kyrios* in place of the divine name (Yahweh which was written, and *adhonai* which was pronounced in its place), they completed the argument: Jesus is Lord, and Yahweh is Lord; therefore Jesus must be divine. This is a somewhat muddled argument, and is no longer as secure as was thought.

In the first place, it now seems clear that *mar* in Aramaic and *adhon* in Hebrew could both be used naturally for human lords and for God. In *Jesus the Jew*, G. Vermes has argued that it is quite likely that even in his own lifetime, Jesus as a highly impressive and charismatic character was regarded as 'lord' by his disciples. Secondly, the Septuagint argument is an odd one and proves too much, for no one in the early church wanted to equate Jesus with Yahweh. They did want to say he was divine, but they avoided bald identification. There is also doubt whether early Jewish copies of the Septuagint really did replace *Yahweh* with *kyrios*, and in any case the matter is complicated rather than illuminated by Septuagintal usage (it is worth noting too that in Old Testament quotations the New Testament uses *kyrios* for Yahweh). It is instructive to read again 1 Corinthians 8:5–6, where Paul in calling Jesus 'lord' seems to distinguish him from Yahweh, the one God. The basic trouble is that all the terms for 'lord' are capable of a range of meaning, and that we need to look beyond the vocabulary to the statements actually made about Jesus *kyrios*.

Invocation and Acclamation

Perhaps there is something in the old distinction between invoking Jesus as (a not necessary divine) lord, and acclaiming him as a divine lord. This suggestion was made because in 1 Corinthians 16:22 Jesus is invoked: the Aramaic phrase *marana tha* means 'Lord, come!' The phrase shows that in the Palestinian, Aramaic-speaking church Jesus was thought of as lord, and that both the fact and this expression of it were well enough known for Paul to include such foreign words in a letter to non-Aramaic speakers. Yet the meaning of *maran* here need not include divinity, for Jesus is simply called on to return and finish his work, at the End, or conceivably in the eucharist, or both. It is obviously a lofty title, but not necessarily divine, and can thus be claimed as a primitive usage.

In the same letter, in 1 Corinthians 8:5–6, we have a quite different – or so it is claimed – use of 'lord', in which Christ is not asked to come, but is acclaimed as the reigning one here and now,

... for us there is only one God, the Father, from whom are all things and for whom we live, and only one Lord, Jesus Christ, through whom are all things and through whom we live.

This sounds as Greek as 16:22 sounds Jewish, yet both are in the same letter, and both are within about 20 years of the

61

historical Jesus. In the second passage, Christ is not only a present rather than a future lord, he is lord of everything without exception, subject only to God the Father. He is a cosmic lord. Thus if there was a development from invocation to acclamation, it happened very early indeed.

Yet even in the second passage there is a reservation. Jesus is bracketed with God, yet clearly distinguished from him: there are gods and there are lords, and the Father is God while Christ is Lord; all things may be *through* Christ, but they are *from* god. The acclamation is therefore not a matter of granting straightforward divine status; it is more nuanced than that, yet at the same time Jesus Christ is certainly no longer a purely human figure. Even 1 Corinthians 16:22 probably precludes that. Another notable 'acclamation' passage is Philippians 2:6–11, which may be a pre-Pauline hymn, in which case it may be startlingly early. Here, on some readings of it, we have a pre-existent Christ who, because of his obedience and willingness to suffer, has been exalted by God to receive 'the name that is above every name', usually taken to be *kyrios* (2:11). Moreover, language that in Isaiah 45:23 is used of Yahweh, is here used of Jesus (though in Romans 14:11 it is used of God),

every knee should bow ... and every tongue confess ...

It appears that Jesus is being put in the place of Yahweh, yet once again there is a reservation: every tongue confesses the lordship of Jesus Christ – to the glory of God the Father! He has the name above every name – because God gives it to him. The note of subordination is insistent.

Thus, very high honours are paid to Jesus Christ early in the New Testament period, honours which seem to be divine, but with a substantial reservation usually called 'subordination'. Again, acclamation and invocation are not the same thing, yet appear in the same (early) Pauline letter. Some sort of development is going on, but what? The small part of the evidence we have already examined warns us to be ready for scholarly disagreement.

Theories about Kyrios
We have as the fundamental issue the question whether there was a distinct change in understanding, or a development along an already existing line. As we should expect, the conceptual background is crucial.

1. Oscar Cullmann, in his *Christology of the New Testament* (1959), having rightly decided that *marana tha* in 1 Corinthians 16:22 shows that Jesus was invoked as lord in the very early, Aramaic-speaking church, concluded that he was in effect addressed and even worshipped as divine almost from the resurrection onwards (chapter 7). There really was no development of christology except perhaps in moving from Semitic to Hellenistic terminology. The essentials of divine honours were there from the start. It must, however, be said that Cullmann sees things largely in functional not in status terms.

2. A more common scholarly position is that of Ferdinand Hahn, in *The Titles of Jesus in Christology* (1969), who sees a decided difference between invoking Jesus to come (as Son of man, or messiah), and acclaiming him as a heavenly, divine, regnant lord. The first stage we can see in *marana tha*, and in the many passages where Jesus is seen as future judge, e.g. Matthew 25:31–46. With the passage of time, and with meditation on Psalm 110:1 ('The Lord says to my lord, "Sit at my right hand, until I make your enemies your footstool"'), Christians began to think less of Christ's future coming as lord, and more of his present lordship in heaven. The church's response then moves from expectation to acknowledgement, obedience, and even worship.

Hahn thinks that Cullmann has telescoped these two distinct stages, the first of which is basically the Palestinian, and the second the Hellenistic. The first is also a christology of function, and the second one of nature, or status. The first is still within the framework of Jesus' eschatology (concern with the End), but the second is a matter of the governance of the cosmos. That the same term, *kyrios*, can be used in both stages shows how perilous it is to assume that a word has one meaning which can be supplied everywhere, for

63

in fact the meanings in the two stages are substantially different.

3. C. F. D. Moule in *The Origin of Christology* (1977) argues that this pulling apart of the two stages is artificial, and that invocation of a future lord, and acclamation of an already exalted one, cannot in practice be neatly distinguished. The two stages run together, for as soon as we speak of a lord who will come to judge, he has already been given an implicit status – for who but Yahweh can judge? Others argue also that in, for example, Acts 3:20 there is no sharp distinction between future judge and presently exalted lord, and moreover that it was the Jewish habit to think of future persons and realities that are part of God's design as already existing in heaven (this is one of the characteristics of that rather cryptic way of talking about the future that we call 'apocalyptic'). Even in the use of Psalm 110:1, there would be strong pressure to see the lord as already being what he was going to be, and it is further clear from 1 Corinthians that both 'stages' co-existed very early indeed – compare 16:22 with 8:5–6.

Assessment

Moule and others have undoubtedly pointed to grave weaknesses in the 'evolutionary' model, so that we cannot lightly talk of the Hellenistic church as having radically altered the understanding of Jesus Christ. It is doubtful whether we can plot *any* straightforward development, however, whether we mean a change of direction or simply an unfolding of implications. At what point we move from veneration of Jesus as an exalted figure, but not divine, to giving him divine honours in some (what?) sense, is appallingly difficult to discover. Too often we do not know in what sense a word is used. What we probably can say with some confidence is that within about 20 years, Christians were regarding Christ as nothing less than God's vice-gerent (see 1 Cor. 8:5f; Phil. 2:6–11; then later Col.1:15–20; Acts 2:33–6; Matt. 28:18; John 1:3). Does this mean that he is God, or was its very ambiguity part of the reason *kyrios* was so much used?

Notes on Books

Introduction
  C. F. D. Moule, *The Origin of Christology*, Cambridge University Press, 1977
Jewish Beginnings, and Hellenistic Developments
  E. Lohse, *The New Testament Environment*, SCM Press, 1976
Hellenistic Judaism
  M. Hengel, *Judaism and Hellenism*, 2 vols., SCM Press, 1974
  R. H. Fuller, *The Foundations of New Testament Christology*, Lutterworth Press, 1965
  Lohse as above
The Issue of Development or Fundamental Change
  F. Hahn, *The Titles of Jesus in Christology*, Lutterworth Press, 1969
  I. H. Marshall, *The Origins of New Testament Christology*, Inter-Varsity Press, 1977, ch. 2
  G. B. Caird, 'The Development of the Doctrine of Christ in the New Testament', in N. Pittenger, (ed.), *Christ for Us Today*, SCM Press, 1968, pp. 66–80
  Fuller and Hengel as above
Jesus Christ is Lord
  G. Vermes, *Jesus the Jew*, Collins, 1973, ch. 5
  Marshall as above, ch. 6
  Moule as above, pp. 35–46
Invocation and Acclamation
  Hahn as above, ch. 2
Theories about *Kyrios*
  O. Cullmann, *Christology of the New Testament*, SCM Press, 1959, ch. 7
  E. Schweizer, *Jesus*, SCM Press, 1971, chs. 3 and 4
  Hahn and Moule as above

5. Does the New Testament say that Jesus is God?

In the previous chapter we saw that quite quickly the church came to a more-than-human estimate of Jesus, though it is often impossible to decide whether that estimate makes him an exalted human being, an angel, or actually divine. We must now ask the direct question about his divinity in the New Testament, and one thing must be said at the outset: the church never has equated Jesus with Yahweh, nor has it ever proposed the reversible equation, Jesus is God and God is Jesus. Whatever we find in the New Testament is unlikely to be as simple as that. Moreover, calling Christ 'divine' is only half way to the answer, if the reversible equation is ruled out, for the meaning of the statement is far from obvious. It is possible, for instance, that early Hellenistic Christians who called Jesus divine simply meant that he was a very remarkable person with an unusually large measure of the divine in him.

We also saw that *kyrios* is a somewhat puzzling title, and hinted that its ambiguity may have been part of its attraction: it established Christ's authority over the believer without attempting to define his nature or his status in relation to God. Yet the authority met in Christ was understood to be ultimate, divine authority, and he was increasingly seen as lord not only of believer and church, but of the cosmos too. Our present question is thus inescapable, but the evidence is alas not straightforward. Despite what is often thought, Jesus is not represented in the gospels as having gone about claiming to be God, though he is recorded as having said some things that point in that direction. However, the evidence does not all point in the same direction, for there are other statements that put him firmly subordinate to God, and as we have seen, when Jesus is given a lofty position or high authority, he is *given* it, by God.

Again, we have seen that within a generation or two Jesus was believed to have been – and to be – God's vice-gerent, and that he was now exalted lord. Perhaps how such beliefs were understood depended on the sort of God that was believed in, and what we said in the previous chapter about Jewish, Hellenistic, and Hellenistic Jewish ideas must be taken as the background to this chapter as well. Is God the sort of being who can share his nature with another? This is the nub of the debate. We must now look at some important passages in the New Testament.

Explicit Statements

There are some places where, in older translations, the New Testament seems to equate Jesus with God, but where this is a misreading for one reason or another or where inferior manuscripts were being followed. Thus it is not now usually claimed that Romans 9:5, 1 Timothy 3:16, or Titus 2:13 call Jesus God. There are some passages whose interpretation is in dispute, such as 2 Peter 1:1, 1 John 5:20, and John 1:18 (where our earliest manuscript reads 'the only-begotten *God*', not 'the only-begotten son'). The late Vincent Taylor in an important article in 1962 in effect gave a negative answer to his question 'Does the New Testament Call Jesus "God"?' The only real exception he allowed was the cry of Thomas in John 20:28 ('My lord and my God'), which Taylor saw as the language of devotion and theologically only one aspect of the christology of John. He argued that in the New Testament period Jewish monotheism was too strong for Jesus to be called God.

Taylor's case probably cannot stand. More recently R. E. Brown, in *Jesus God and Man* (1968), has shown that there is a small group of passages in which Jesus is called God, but they all belong to the latter end of the New Testament period. As we should expect, confessing Jesus as not just superhuman or highly exalted, but actually God, belongs to a late stage of

67

the primitive church. Thus the three passages above that I called 'in dispute' are rejected by Taylor but accepted by Brown. Unlike Taylor, Brown also thinks that Hebrews 1:8-9, in which a passage from Psalm 45 is applied to Jesus, does identify him as divine, though it is rather problematic because the second part of the quotation seems to say that Yahweh is the God *of* Christ. Brown finds the evidence from John's gospel unambiguous. In John 20:28, the confession of Thomas, which Taylor also was obliged to admit, the clarity and downrightness seem to outdo anything else in the New Testament; Paul in 1 Corinthians 8:6 had distinguished the Father as God from Christ as lord, and even in Philippians 2:6-11 and Colossians 2:9 the distinction is maintained, but here in John 20:28 there is no such distinction. There is of course discussion about the confession's background: is it parallel to calling Yahweh 'the lord God' in the Old Testament? Or is it an echo of the claims of the late first century Emperor Domitian, who liked to be addressed as 'my lord and my god'? The second would make it a less lofty ascription than the first, for to be classed with Yahweh is vastly different from being classed with Domitian! Nevertheless, Jesus is clearly called God in this verse, as he is in John 1:18 according to some manuscripts, and in John 1:1,

'the Word was with God and the Word was God'.

In John 1 the Word (*Logos*) is Christ, which implies that here he is called God, surely? Not quite, for if there is a simple equation, how can the Word be *with* God? Are there two Gods? It was doubtless for reasons like this as well as on grammatical grounds (there is in the Greek an article before *Logos* but not one before God), that the New English Bible translators decided to render the statement 'what God was the Word was'. This is puzzling, but at least it says neither too much nor too little, and brings out the oddity that there is in the Greek.

It seems, then, that mainly in books usually dated late among New Testament writings (John, 1 John, 2 Peter, and perhaps Hebrews), Jesus is called divine and is not just a human or even superhuman figure. Yet in every case the assertion or confession has something odd and qualifying about it. Even in John 20:28, we need to remember that three verses later Jesus is called not God but the Son of God, and that ten verses earlier he speaks about 'my God'. There is still no simple equation of Jesus with God.

The Understanding of Christ in the Fourth Gospel

There is a good deal in John which puts Jesus on the divine side of the line between God and man.

The Father and I are one (10:30) – which does *not* say 'I am the Father'!

He that has seen me has seen the Father (14:9).

I am in the Father and the Father in me (14:11); moreover, when Jesus says 'I am . . .' in 8:24, 28, 58, and 13:19, it sounds very much as if this is a deliberate attempt to echo the Old Testament name of Yahweh (see Exodus 3:14).

Again, according to 17:5, Jesus shared God's glory before creation, and the way Jesus calls God his Father is taken by his opponents (5:18) to be tantamount to making himself equal with God, and this is not denied. Jesus exhibits 'glory' (2:11), the usual way of indicating the veiled presence of God.

All this – and there is more – seems naturally to lead to the view brilliantly propounded by E. Käsemann in *The Testament of Jesus* (1968) that in John's interpreted picture of Jesus, he is quite simply God, and not man at all. His humanity is only apparent ('docetic'), for Jesus is a divine visitant in disguise. The fact that he appears to be human merely shows the effectiveness of the disguise. He is really God, though not Yahweh; rather, in the Hellenistic manner, he is both the representative of and a sort of extension of the ultimate God. He is not, to speak absurdly, the whole of God, but he is divine and certainly not truly human. Käsemann thinks 1:14 ('the Word was made flesh . . .') is part of an appendage added to the prologue later and is not its climax, nor is it to be taken as the key to John's understanding of Jesus. Käsemann does not, of course, think that Jesus really was like this, but sees it as John's theological interpretation of Jesus.

Is he right? Many scholars, such as R. E. Brown in his massive commentary on the Fourth Gospel, consider that Käsemann makes too little of the delicate balance of statements in John. We could draw up a quite different list giving a different perspective from that of Käsemann, including these, 'the Son can do nothing of his own accord, but only what he sees the Father do' (5:19); his teaching is not his own, 'but his who sent me' (7:16); 'the Father is greater than I am' (14:28); he has kept the Father's commandments, and so the Father loves him (15:10). The message is clear: Jesus is strictly subordinate to the Father. Jesus is seen by John as the Father's agent, representative, vice-gerent and almost plenipotentiary, with the result that to a large extent things that can be said about God can also be said about Jesus. This does not infringe, on the contrary it requires, Jesus' status as a subordinate figure distinct from God, to whom he prays and indeed of whom he speaks as a third party.

In John therefore, on the one hand Jesus is pre-existent and of equal standing with God, and on the other he is human and called by lofty but unmistakably human titles like 'messiah' (1:41, 49) and 'prophet' (4:44; cf. 6:14; 7:40). Moreover, Käsemann's proposal to regard 1:14 ('And the Word became flesh ...') as a later addition and not integral to John's thinking has found as much disagreement as support. Jesus as a real human being is important to the Fourth Gospel. Thus while Käsemann correctly stresses half the picture, half is what it is widely taken to be.

There are two particular ways in which John's understandings of Christ is focused: his use of the expressions 'Son' and 'Son of God', and his use of the 'Logos' idea. To these we now turn.

Jesus as Son of God in John's Gospel
It is not certain that 'Son' (as correlative to 'Father') and 'Son of God' are used in the same way, but it is difficult to maintain a consistent distinction and I shall take the two expressions together. What is meant by 'Son of God'? It is so common in Christian usage that its metaphorical or analogical nature is

easily forgotten, and we too easily assume that somehow or other it explains things, but in fact it is a very odd way of speaking – God cannot have a son in the usual sense. The strangeness is compounded by the fact that in New Testament times the expression could mean a number of different things, and it is not easy to work out what it means in any given place. In the Old Testament and traditional Judaism, the term could often be used for the nation of Israel (e.g. Hosea 11:1), or for a representative of the nation, like a king (e.g. Psalm 2:7). The point was that like a good son, nation and king were commissioned by God and would obediently do what he wanted. The first thing about a son in ancient Judaism was that he did what his father wanted, though it cannot be denied that special status is also involved, for a son is not a slave. This status, however, did not entail any identity between god and nation or God and individual (whether the individual was a king, a prophet, or – by the first century BC – a righteous sufferer as in the apocryphal Wisdom of Solomon 2:10–20 and 5:1–5). A son of God was certainly not divine.

There are aspects of John's use of the term which fit all this rather well, notably the stress on commission and obedience, 'the Father has sent me'. Of course this is balanced by a note of intimacy, particularly in chapter 17 where there is perhaps a spelling out of what is implied in the 'Abba' address in Mark 14:36. Nevertheless the undeniably special relationship between Jesus and the Father is emphatically not an exclusive one, for the oneness between them is intended as a pioneering oneness which will embrace believers also (cf. 14:20; 15:7; 17:11, 23, 26), just as Paul sees the 'Abba' address as now open to believers too (Gal. 4:4ff; Rom. 8:15).

The term could be taken in a more Hellenistic sense, to mean a human being in whom there is an unusually large element of divinity as demonstrated by miraculous powers. Indeed part of the reason for the scholarly debate as to whether the Fourth Gospel belongs to a Jewish or a Hellenistic milieu is this very point – how should we read 'Son of God'? However if we read through chapter 6, for example, it does seem tolerably clear that for John the term has very strong agent and function connotations, together with a strong emphasis on communion between Son and Father. The matter of pre-existence is also raised in this connection, but we shall look at that after considering the other focus of christology in John.

Christ as the Logos of God

'Son of God' is far from being a peculiarly Johannine designation for Jesus, though it is perhaps less prominent elsewhere. *Logos* ('word') on the other hand appears explicitly only in John 1, though it is perhaps implied in 1 John 1:1 and something like it lies behind Hebrews 1:1–4. What does it mean? We have an embarrassment of possible backgrounds, for John is usually seen as at the meeting of two worlds. It is possible to explain the prologue (i.e. 1:1–18) in more or les Stoic terms, with the Logos as the divine reason, the rational principle which keeps the universe together and makes it comprehensible to the rational mind, but which has now been revealed not in cosmic order or rationality but in the life of the man Jesus. It is likely that the basic idea owes more to the contemporary notion, especially in Hellenistic Judaism, of *wisdom* as both a characteristic of God from the beginning, and also God's active agent who descends from God to reveal and save.

It is possible however that it should be understood in more Old Testament terms: God's Logos, his Word, is his creative self-communication and self-expression which is part of his very nature, and naturally was there from the beginning. It existed before creation, and indeed creation 'by the Word' means that the creation is an expression of God (cf. Genesis 1, where God creates solely by his word). Before creation, this Logos or self-expression could only be reflexive, towards himself, hence it was simply 'with God', or literally 'towards God' (1:1). Now, however, this same Logos is seen in a radically new form, neither in words nor in the structure of the cosmos, but in a specific human life. The message is a person, a genuinely human person just as the world is a real world and a prophet's words are genuinely human words, though all are of divine origin. As the expression of God, the

Logos is divine, is God himself in his revelation. Like those who belong to him (1:13), Jesus has his origin in the will of God, not of man – as of course in Jewish thought does the Torah, also the Logos of God. For John, Jesus is now the decisive place where God speaks, and the Torah, the Law, is superseded.

It does seem likely that behind John's Logos idea lies the Jewish and Hellenistic-Jewish idea of *Wisdom*, and that the 'Wisdom-myth' is used by him as the vehicle for his teaching at this point. In the Old Testament, notably in Proverbs 1–9, Wisdom is not just an attribute of God, but is talked of in near-personal terms, as an entity carrying out God's will and communicating God's truth to men (see especially Proverbs 8:1–31), which existed before creation. This figure appears often enough in later Jewish literature to suggest that it was a common way of thinking about God's self-revelation and dealings with the world. In the apocryphal book Sirach (or Ecclesiasticus) 24, Wisdom has come from the mouth of God, has descended to earth and is found throughout the world, but cannot find a resting-place except with Israel, for all other peoples reject her. This is how it is that God's truth comes to Israel alone. In Wisdom of Solomon 7, Wisdom has apparently become almost another being alongside God, though of course deriving from him, who was his agent in creation and is his agent in revelation for those who will receive her (see also chapter 8). The myth of Wisdom as the figure who descends to give God's revelation but who is rejected and finally returns to heaven, is found also in Ethiopian Enoch 42, and is probably connected with the speculations about an original *anthropos* (man) which we find in Philo of Alexandria. This heavenly *anthropos*-figure is rather elusive, but in at least some traditions there was the story of the figure who would descend to earth to restore in himself the brokenness of a humanity which had fallen away from its primaeval wholeness and perfection.

Most of this thinking took place in Hellenistic Judaism, and is widely thought to have provided the framework in which Christ could be understood in Christian circles belonging to that milieu. The links with the Logos doctrine are obvious. Just as the Wisdom figure was not seen as a threat to the unity of God, no more was the Logos, for as God's self-communication it is not really another entity alongside God, but God himself in action. None the less this does raise the question how far this language was taken literally, how far Wisdom was a personification, just a way of speaking, and how far it was seen as an independent being. In Christian terms, how far can the incarnate Logos be seen as an independent reality, and how far as simply an expression or revelation of God? The problems are enormous, yet in the light of all that we have seen, the basic point being made by John's Logos doctrine is probably very simple: Jesus conveys God, both in revelation and in action.

Except in a very few places such as 1:18, the 'Son' language and the 'Logos' language are kept apart by John, and Logos does not appear in the body of the gospel, where Son of God is common. Throughout the gospel the distinction between God and Jesus is made very clear, and in number they are two, not one. Yet there appears to be identity of function, this being conveyed not only by 'Logos' and 'Son' languages, but also by such specific statements as 5:19: the Son does nothing of his own will, but always and only what the Father does and wants. It is probably in this sense that he who has seen Jesus has seen the Father (14:9 – see the stress on function in the ensuing verses). How to sort all this out was a major pre-occupation of the church for more than three centuries, for it was the Fourth Gospel's teaching which provided the main source-material for the theological debates. The two chief problems were those of the relation of Christ, as Logos and Son, to God (i.e. the problem of the unity of God), and of the relation of the divine and human in Jesus Christ (i.e. the problem of christology). We shall concentrate on the second, though the first was equally important, and the two are closely interconnected. Later Christian doctrine was an attempt to make coherent sense out of the apparently conflicting and certainly puzzling materials in the New Testament generally, and in John especially. What it is important not to do is to start reading the later solutions and doctrines into John's gospel, or into any other New Testament writings.

The Pre-existence of Christ

A key issue in sorting out just what is being said about Christ is the question of when he began. We saw that in its later stages the New Testament does on a few occasions say that Jesus is God, and we have just seen that in the Logos teaching John claims that Christ is an expression or self-communication of God in a human life. Surely this means that in some fashion Jesus Christ, far from beginning in the first century AD, had no beginning? We may seem to have travelled a long way from our historical discussion of the alleged political aims of Jesus, as indeed we have, yet this journey was taken within a generation or two of the crucifixion. I am not talking only about John 1, but about such passages as 1 Corinthians 8:6, Colossians 1:15–20, and perhaps Philippians 2:6–11. Christ is seen as having a cosmic role in the creation and sustaining of the universe, as well as having been pre-existent. Some see further evidence in passages like 1 Corinthians 10, where Paul seems to say that Christ was with Israel in the wilderness.

Before we conclude that in all this we have deserted history and gone over to mythology, there are three things that must be said.

1. Pre-existence in itself is not the same as divinity. For modern man, being pre-existent probably is incompatible with genuine humanness because of our view of man as being formed out of the contributions of genes and chromosomes from two parents. For first-century man, and especially for a first-century Jew, this was not so, and a number of things were thought of as pre-existent without their being divine. The Torah (Law), the Temple, Wisdom of course, and even Moses were all spoken of in this way, and certainly Moses was never thought to have been divine.

2. This leads us to our second caution. In Jewish circles, and not just in Hellenistic Jewish ones, it was natural and not

uncommon to ascribe pre-existence to anything that was regarded as particularly important religiously. God was even depicted as studying the pre-existent Torah, and using it when planning the Temple, which was itself regarded as pre-existent. If Jesus is a more decisive word from God even than the Torah, then it is necessary and inevitable that he too should be described as pre-existent; otherwise he would be ranked below it. It is in deliberate contrast to Jewish pre-existent entities that this is claimed for Jesus.

3. We must ask yet again how literally such language is to be taken. This question is near the centre of much contemporary theological debate as it is of New Testament interpretation. Just what do the words mean? Do they really refer to foreknowledge and then foreordination by God? Are they essentially a way of stressing importance and the divine *design* behind it all? Or do they literally mean what they say, that Christ existed alongside God from all eternity? If the last, then how can God be one, and how can Christ be human? The problem has not been made easier by the fact that R. G. Hamerton-Kelly seems to have shown that in Judaism not all pre-existent things are in the same category, which means the issue is even more open than was thought. In fact there is at present no secure way of determining how such language was understood where there is no definite indication in the text.

What we can say is that it would be surprising if pre-existence had not been ascribed to Jesus, and that the use of the 'Wisdom' figure to express his significance made it inevitable that the ascription should happen. How far such language really tries to say something about the personal history of Christ, and how far it is a mythological or metaphorical way of speaking of his significance and of God's endorsement of him, is another matter. Probably a further influence on the understanding of Jesus was the habit in apocalyptic thought of speaking of future realities as already existing, prepared in heaven. This is most readily observed by Christian readers in the Book of Revelation (or *Apocalypse*) in which the future is seen by looking into heaven now. The

76

early Christians who saw themselves as at a key point in an apocalyptic drama would naturally suppose that the Christ who had been sent to them, and who would return, had for long ages existed in heaven with God.

Finally there is the question of who or what is said to be pre-existent, a question to which there is no clear answer. Obviously God is pre-existent, and therefore the God who acts, speaks, and reveals himself in Jesus Christ is preexistent. The Logos was from the beginning. Does this or does it not mean that the historical individual, Jesus, was preexistent? We shall need to return to this matter later, but may note in the meantime the view once expressed by G. B. Caird, that so far as the New Testament is concerned, it is only with Paul in 2 Corinthians 8:9 and Philippians 2:6–7 that we have an explicit statement that the concrete person, Jesus Christ, was pre-existent, and that this is a mark of how overwhelmed Paul was by that person.

Conclusion

The New Testament does, rarely, call Jesus God, and more often implicitly puts him on the divine side of the line, without explaining what this means. The 'Wisdom' imagery in which the church expressed its estimate of Jesus meant that both pre-existence and divinity (in some sense) were bound to be ascribed to him. We have found it impossible to come to sharp categorical statements about his position and nature, and have perhaps also begun to see why the church debated such matters for centuries, with all sides claiming to give the correct interpretation of the New Testament. Of course these problems would not have arisen for the church if she had been ready to say that Jesus was not truly human, or ready to concede plurality in the divine, with perhaps one deity superior and another inferior. Instead, she went on insisting that God was one and indivisible, and that Jesus really was a man, and so was in time driven at councils like those of Nicaea and Chalcedon to make the attempt to deal with the questions of unity and trinity in God, and of humanity and divinity in Christ.

Notes on Books

Explicit Statements

V. Taylor, 'Does the New Testament call Jesus "God"?' in *New Testament Essays*, Epworth Press, 1970, pp. 83–89

R. E. Brown, *Jesus God and Man*, Geoffrey Chapman, 1968, pp. 1–38

The Understanding of Christ in the Fourth Gospel

E. Käsemann, *The Testament of Jesus*, SCM Press, 1968

C. K. Barrett, *The Gospel According to St John*, 2nd edn, SPCK, 1978, pp.70–75 and appropriate verses

R. E. Brown, *The Gospel According to John*, 2 vols., Geoffrey Chapman, 1971, sections IV and VIII of the Introduction to Vol. I. and appropriate verses

Jesus as Son of God in John's Gospel

M. Hengel, *The Son of God*, SCM Press, 1976

O. Cullmann, *The Christology of the New Testament*, SCM Press, 1959, ch.10

The commentaries of Brown and Barrett as above

Christ as the Logos of God

T. E. Pollard, *Johannine Christology in the Early Church*, Cambridge University Press, 1970, especially ch.1

M. Hengel, *Judaism and Hellenism*, 2 vols., SCM Press, 1974

R. H. Fuller, *The Foundations of New Testament Christology*, Lutterworth Press 1965, especially pp. 72–8

R. G. Hamerton-Kelly, *Pre-existence, Wisdom, and the Son of Man*, Cambridge University Press, 1973

The commentaries of Barrett and Brown, especially in the latter Vol. I, Appendix II

Hengel, *The Son of God*, ch. 5

The Pre-existence of Christ

Hengel, *Judaism and Hellenism*, especially Vol. I pp. 155–60, 233–50

G. B. Caird, 'The Development of the Doctrine of Christ in the New Testament', in N. Pittenger, (ed.), *Christ for Us Today*, SCM Press, 1968, pp. 66–80

J. Knox, *The Humanity and Divinity of Christ*, Cambridge University Press, 1967, especially pp. 10–11, 21–22.
Hamerton-Kelly as above.
All these matters are discussed in most books about christology, such as those already listed by F. Hahn, I. H. Marshall, N. Pittenger, G. Vermes, and a very good lucid introduction is now provided in
Neil Richardson, *Was Jesus Divine?* Epworth Press, 1979

6. Does the New Testament regard Jesus as truly human?

The human Jesus persists in early Christian writings not only because of memory, common sense, and a desire for historical accuracy, but also because developing theology needed a truly human figure. In our day Christian piety may often start not from the human Jesus but from the divine lord, but we may be sure that this was not so for the very earliest believers. For them, the real humanness of Jesus was to be taken for granted, and did not need to be asserted. Yet before long it does begin to be disputed, and in 1 John 4:2 we find polemic against those who deny his humanity. It is surprising that a human Jesus survived at all, when you consider the developments we have been following in the last two chapters.

Jesus was a Real Man

Although the Synoptic gospels (Matthew, Mark, and Luke) were all written long after Jesus had begun to be regarded as the Wisdom of God, and as exalted Lord, they all portray an unmistakably human figure. The case of John is more difficult, for even if we reject Käsemann's picture of an only apparently human Johannine Christ, it is true that he comes trailing very distinct clouds of glory. Nevertheless, in the Synoptics three significantly different forms of the human figure persist, perhaps because the traditions of his words and actions maintained it even when confession ('Jesus is Lord!') and worship had gone beyond it. Jesus is a man, a person.

It would be tiresome and unnecessary to list all the passages which stress or assume that Jesus is human. He accepts the religious customs of his time and nation. He is involved in a network of relationships with friends and family. He has enemies, about whom he can be harsh. He eats and drinks, rather more than some think proper. He sleeps, even at inconvenient moments. He weeps, and recoils from suffering. All these and more are found throughout the gospel material. No attempt is made to *establish* his humanity, because it is taken for granted. Thus when he is crucified, it is for playing politics, a very human activity. Above all, he dies.

We have seen how difficult it is to discern how Jesus saw himself, and probably we cannot go further than James Dunn, who thinks he was aware of a distinctive and unique vocation, and of God's presence and power in him and his ministry (*Jesus and the Spirit*, Part I, especially pp. 88–92). It was later supposed that he went about knowing himself to be the second person of the trinity, but this is an interpretation of the gospel picture, not that picture itself. Even in the fourth gospel, no such thing is said. He is depicted as having an intimate relationship with God to whom he frequently prays, but in praying he is undoubtedly put on the human side of the line.

Jesus is shown on occasion as lacking knowledge (e.g. Mark 13:32) and it is astonishing that any trace of this is allowed to remain in the tradition, for before long he was to be credited with all the knowledge God has. Luke 2:52 says quite calmly that, like all other human beings, Jesus had to develop. Now it is also true that on some occasions Jesus is portrayed as having extraordinary insight and foresight: thus he predicts his passion (Mark 8:31; 9:31; 10:33f), but while the details may have been supplied with hindsight by the church, the fact that he expected to be rejected and killed is neither improbable nor at odds with genuine humanity. It points to his ability to read the consequences of his own actions, like Martin Luther King, who also foresaw his own death. Some sort of telepathic awareness is credited to him in John's gospel, cf. 1:47–51, 4:17f, 6:61, 16:19, and also see Mark 10:21. Jesus is no ordinary man, yet he is a man, and alongside such extraordinary knowledge lies his ignorance, including his expectation of the great consummation in the near future, about which he was mistaken. That he did have this expectation is shown by such notable passages as Matthew 10:23 and Mark 9:1.

On other matters Jesus was a man of his time. It is seldom now seriously believed that he was aware of molecular biology or nuclear physics or the existence of the American continent. He lived in a flat earth, somewhat infested by evil spirits. Generally speaking, he knew only what a first-century man in his circumstances could know, and to affirm the contrary goes beyond the evidence of the gospels and denies his humanness. He did, according to the gospels, know *God* in an unprecedented way, but this does not interfere with normal human knowledge and ignorance of *things* (the best recent treatment of these matters is in chapter 2 of R. E. Brown, *Jesus God and Man*).

The very great *powers* evident in the ministry of Jesus according to all the gospels, need not threaten his humanity, for they are God's power working in and through him (see for example Matt. 12:28/Luke 11:20, and even John 14:10). Let it be said again that Jesus was by any standards no ordinary man, but an extraordinary, charismatic, prophetic, powerful character. Yet nothing so far is incompatible with his being one of us, born of woman, born under the Law (Gal. 4:4).

Of all New Testament books, it is the Letter to the Hebrews which again and again underlines how important it is that this should be so. Jesus, now exalted as High Priest and Intercessor, was *one of us*, and had he not been, he could not act as our heavenly representative nor as the pioneer, the trailblazer, of *our* way to God.

> He had to be made like his brothers in every way (Hebrews 2:17, cf. 2:10, 11, 14).
> For because he himself has been tempted and has suffered, he is able to help those who are tempted (2:18, cf. also 5:2).
> We do not have a high priest who cannot suffer with our weaknesses, but one who in every way has been tempted like us, but without sinning (4:15, cf. 5:1ff).

82

Although he was a son, he learned obedience through what he suffered (5:8, cf. also 5:7); being perfected, he became the source of eternal salvation... (5:9).

The whole passage, 4:14 – 5:10, is highly instructive. There is nothing naïve or unreflective here, for in many ways Hebrews has one of the highest (most divine) christologies in the New Testament. On the contrary, it is *theologically* important to the unknown author that Jesus should have been truly human.

Contrary Evidence

Yet is there also reason to think that Jesus was not seen as a real man? In the gospels, the obvious piece of relevant evidence is the story of the virginal conception in its two (Lukan and Matthaean) versions. (Following R. E. Brown I take 'virginal conception' to mean that Jesus was conceived without the participation of a human male, and 'virgin birth' to mean that Mary was still a virgin at the time of the birth of Jesus.) Men as we know them are not born of virgins, so how can this story be compatible with humanness? A lot depends on how the story – which is peripheral to the New Testament, being reflected nowhere else, not even in the body of the two gospels concerned – is understood. Miraculous births in ancient thought were not necessarily taken to imply the divinity of the child, though it would certainly be expected to be out of the ordinary: we may think of Isaac in the Old Testament, and Gotama in Buddhist tradition. Ancient Hellenistic man was accustomed to the notion that gods fathered children by human mothers, the issue then being literally demi-gods, but this, despite some parallels often adduced, is not what Matthew and Luke describe. They tell rather of the action of the Holy Spirit in conception, so that instead of the usual two human parents, Jesus has only his mother plus that action. There are difficulties in reconciling this with the doctrine that he was God's Son from all eternity, for here he comes into existence only at his birth, but the church found ways of effecting a reconciliation, notably in the 'two natures' doctrine which we shall come to later.

As it stands, it must have been understood by ordinary people in the Hellenistic world as making Jesus a demi-god, the Son of God because God was literally his Father. Although the story is not as simple and crude as that, it is a considerable barrier against seeing Jesus as a real man with normal genetic equipment. But perhaps we ought not to and were never meant to take the story so literally; perhaps it is a way of stressing the divine initiative in the life and being of Jesus, and a way of stating the divine significance of his human life. Certainly some, like J. A. T. Robinson in *The Human Face of God* (chapter 2), argue that in both Matthew and Luke we have stories on two levels: on the human level, Jesus is the child of Joseph and Mary, and this is represented by the genealogies both of which trace his lineage through the supposedly irrelevant Joseph; on the other level, which is in effect an interpretation of the first, the origin of Jesus is seen to lie not in a couple of parents, but in the design of God. If he is right, and many agree with him, the virginal conception story is not meant to be taken literally, but as a theological account of the significance of Jesus. Its truth is theological, not biological. Moreover, it is possible that in Luke the birth of Jesus needs to be more remarkable than that of John the Baptist, which is also miraculous, for Jesus is of more significance in God's design than John, and so a virginal conception makes the point. Needless to say, there are many who would accept that the point of the story is theological, but still maintain that it is biologically true. My present point is that it is easier to affirm the full humanity of Jesus if something like Robinson's line is followed.

There are also passages which, if read in the light of their probable Old Testament background, seem to imperil the humanity of Jesus. A notable instance is the story of the stilling of the storm, especially in Mark's version (4:35–41) where there seem to be distinct echoes of Psalm 107:23–32. In Mark, Jesus does what in the Psalm is done by God: he controls the forces of nature. Not unnaturally this raises the question (Mark 4:41) of what sort of being he is who so fully bears the power of God. An answer is not given, but at the least he must be God's vice-gerent, though this does not necessarily prevent his being human.

If there are ways in which we can take such stories as these, and still maintain the humanness of Jesus, what about the sinlessness that is commonly ascribed to him? If to err is human, is not the reverse true, not to err is not to be human?

Jesus as Sinless Man

This is a confusing and delicate issue which needs to be clarified before its bearing on our question can be determined. First, the sinlessness of Jesus is a faith-judgment, not an historical one. I mean that it cannot be tested historically. We can never prove a negative, i.e. that Jesus never sinned, because there could always be a hidden instance and because we never have access to another's mind. We know so little about the words, actions, and thoughts of Jesus that it would be absurd to claim on historical grounds that he was totally sinless. The most we could claim is that we have no evidence that he was sinful. People who base their belief in his divinity on the ground that his earthly life was the best and most beautiful ever lived, are building faith on faith, not faith on history. Many Jews indeed presumably *did* find him sinful.

Secondly, there is the question of definition: what do we mean by sin? Do we mean wrong attitudes as well as wrong actions and words, or do we mean something more basic like a wrong orientation of life? If we include attitudes, what do we make of Matthew 23, where from what we can discover in other sources, we have a one-sided and generalizing condemnation of the Pharisees that is unfair as an overall picture and assumes the worst in detail? If *we* spoke like that, we should be regarded as uncharitable. Most exegetes in fact say that Matthew 23 owes more to the attitude of Matthew and his church than to the historical Jesus, and they are probably right, but how far is this judgment influenced by a prior conviction that anything so unpleasant cannot be ascribed to Jesus? Or, are we more inclined to say that if Jesus said it, it cannot be unkind or unjust despite appearances? Either way, it looks as if we are arranging things to fit our preconceived notion of the sinlessness of Jesus.

A number of writers, including C. F. D. Moule, G. W. H. Lampe, and J. A. T. Robinson, have argued that this is the wrong way to approach the matter of sinlessness, and that what is meant is the whole 'set' of the life of Jesus. If sin is basically a wrong orientation, then the important thing about Jesus is that his orientation was entirely right, towards God and towards obedience. He was totally in harmony with God, and totally open to him. The gospels show, and Paul in particular stresses, that when it mattered and when crucial decisions had to be made, Jesus chose always with and never against God, as when he faced the cross (see Mark 14:32–42, in Gethsemane, and Romans 5:12–21, on his obedience). In this, he was the precise antithesis of Adam, for in him there was no basic estrangement from God, no rebellion.

Thirdly, the sinlessness of Jesus was a theological necessity. Once he was seen as the communication of God in the medium of a human life, or as the unique bearer of God's authority even in purely functional terms, it began to be inconceivable that he should be imperfect. God cannot reveal himself through sin, so how could he tolerate sin in his representative? To allow sin or imperfection in Jesus would be absurd. Moreover, if as for Paul he is the antithesis of Adam, his sinlessness is a crucial part of the antithesis, and we shall say more about this in a moment. For Hebrews, the sinlessness of Jesus is essential, for he is not only High Priest, but also sacrificial victim. In the sacrificial system, only an immaculate victim would do since its function is to cleanse, restore and renew; accordingly Jesus is immaculate (see Hebrews 9:14;10:1–14, and also 1 Peter 1:19). He must be immaculate as High Priest too. In the Temple ritual, the High Priest must cleanse himself before he officiates (5:3), but it is remarkable that this is where the parallel with Jesus breaks down: he does not need to make a sacrifice for his own sins, though in every other respect he is one of us, and so fitted to

86

be our High Priest (4:15). This sinlessness is no mere technicality: because of it he is able to function all the time (7:17) and once for all (7:26-28). Strangely enough, this sinlessness is seen in Hebrews as something achieved, especially by his acceptance of the cross, see especially 5:7-9; 7:28, and also 2:10 and 5:2. The temptations were real (chapter 5) and had to be overcome by a struggle, and it begins to seem that what Hebrews means by sinlessness is what Paul means by obedience in the concrete life of Jesus.

This notion is not an insuperable barrier against his true humanity. Indeed, the New Testament pictures Jesus as conveying in his life the goodness as well as the power of God, but in this he is not to be regarded as fundamentally different from *man as God intends him to be.* The obedient Jesus, with his life 'set' towards God and based entirely on God, is not an anomaly but a paradigm, a model for the human race. This is to see Jesus as future man, as the new image of God replacing Adam who failed to be truly that image. Generally in Paul 'image' refers to Jesus, not Adam, for he and not Adam is the pattern of humanity (see 1 Cor. 15:49; 2 Cor. 3:18; 4:4; Rom. 8:29; also Col. 1:15; 3:10). This brings us to our next point.

Jesus as Corporate Man

This idea of Christ as the new humanity, i.e. as some sort of corporate figure, is almost insuperably difficult for us. We can think of corporate entities like a team, a nation, a college, with which we identify ourselves and our interests, and we can think of representative figures, whether real or mythical, like Britannia, Uncle Sam, or a monarch. What we cannot readily do is conceive of an actual, historical person who is also a corporate entity. Yet Paul, and perhaps other New Testament writers, see Christ as just such a figure.

We may get close to the idea when we recall that in Israel the patriarchs were individuals who also stood for the nation. This was most obviously true of Israel (Jacob) who is both a person and the nation, but there is some evidence that Adam too was seen in a dual way, though as C. F. D. Moule points out (*The Origin of Christology*, p. 52) it is not entirely clear that the notion of the corporate individual is to be found in the Old Testament or Judaism. Perhaps Abraham (cf. Gal. 3:8) is the most plausible case. Whatever the history of the conception, Paul, especially in Romans 5 and 1 Corinthians 15, does see both Adam and Christ as corporate individuals. We are naturally 'in Adam' but are called to become 'in Christ'. These are two sorts of humanity, two ways of being human, and the two representative men, Adam and Christ, are thus much more than historical individuals.

The easiest way to take this sort of language is the Gnostic. We are in Christ literally, for Christ is the original divine humanity which at some pre-historic fall was shattered, and the resulting fragments are now embedded in human beings. Men and women are therefore needed to complete the original man (Christ) and restore his pristine unity and fullness. Believers (Christian Gnostics) are in effect the rest of Christ. I suppose no one believes this sort of thing today, but it is plausible to the extent that it takes for granted that only the divine can be inclusive of others. Yet the initial reference is to Christ as the inclusive *man*, as the parallel with Adam makes certain. As C. F. D. Moule argues, this 'corporate Christ' notion is evidence for a high christology early in the development of Christian thinking (*The Origin of Christology*, chapter 2), but it is noteworthy that it is worked out primarily in human terms. However odd it may seem to us, Paul could think of Christ in human and in corporate terms at the same time. Perhaps (to mix our metaphors) one way of grasping the idea is to think of fields of force as in electro-magnetism, and to see ourselves as living in the field of force of Adam, or in that of Christ. By field of force is meant not only authority (lordship) but also power, dynamism. Adam and Christ, as archetypal heads of different kinds of humanity, wield their authority and exercise their power.

We must take a further step. Although the two humanities are in parallel, for Paul the Christ field of force is that of God. This is not very evident in Romans 5:12–21, though there are hints in verses 15b, 17b, 20b, 21, especially in the references to grace. It is, I think, unavoidable in 1 Corinthians 15, especially in verses 45ff where the last Adam (Christ) becomes 'a life-giving Spirit', and it is implicit in passages like Romans 8 where there appears to be effectively an equivalence between being in Christ and being in the Spirit. This is all of great importance, for it is a case of the divinity rising out of the humanity and being not at all in competition with it. Indeed the divinity requires the humanity, and this non-competitive relationship will be recalled when we examine Schoonenberg's ideas in our final chapter.

Needless to say, Paul does not suppose that Christ was this corporate figure before the resurrection (cf. 'became' in 1 Cor. 15:45, and see also Rom. 6:9ff; the same is probably to be inferred in John's gospel, compare 17:22 with 12:32). The conception entails the point already made, namely that the humanity in Christ is the humanity of the future, the humanity of God's intention, and that for which men and women are destined. Christ's humanity is not his own property only, but is for others who are thus raised to new heights (see for example Hebrews 1:4–5; 1:14–2:10; Col. 1:15–29 and 3:10; Eph. 1:11–23; John 1:13, as well as Rom. 8:29 and 1 Cor. 15:49). Christ's humanity is the ground of others' renewed, transformed, and *true* humanity, which in the end means that what it is to be human is defined by Christ as the true man. Far from his humanity being unreal, it is the most real of all, and what enables ours to be real. To borrow a phrase, Christ is man come of age.

Patterns of Christology

It is time to take stock and ask what all this means for modern man. I hope it is evident that a straightforward identification of Jesus Christ with God is not what the New Testament gives us, and that qualifications and subtleties are unavoidable. Moreover, the genuine humanness of Jesus is not only assumed, it is theologically required: unless he is truly man, crucial things cannot be said. Yet more than human things are said about him quite early in the New Testament period, and we have been trying to see how some of these fit in with the human things. We have had to acknowledge difficulties and uncertainties, and at one point have found that the divinity and humanity may not necessarily be in conflict, and that the first may require the second. This may have caused us to wonder if the common assumption, that humanity and divinity must somehow be fitted together into Jesus Christ as parts of a whole, is really a fruitful one.

Before we move beyond the New Testament, it may help to clarify the position if I refer to the *patterns* of understanding Jesus Christ which have been proposed by John Knox in *The Humanity and Divinity of Christ* (see especially chapter 1). He thinks there are three and only three primitive Christian views.

1. There is the exaltation or 'adoptionist' pattern, probably the earliest. Jesus, a righteous servant of God, killed by wicked men, has been vindicated by God in the resurrection, and is exalted to God's right hand as lord or Christ or both, and will soon return to assume his rightful status. He is a man, who is in effect promoted at the resurrection to superhuman or even divine status. This scheme can be found in Acts 2:36 and many other places, e.g. Romans 10:9; Philippians 2:9; Hebrews 1:3–5 and 5:9–10; Acts 13:33, and may well lie behind Romans 1:3–4. Some think that the future-coming part of the scheme is earlier than the present-exaltation part.

2. In the second scheme the stress is still on the human Jesus who, however, like Wisdom and Torah, existed as an exalted person before as well as after his earthly life. In time it became necessary to explain how such an exalted one could have been a real human being, and the explanation given was that he voluntarily laid aside his heavenly glory, his powers, and (later) his attributes; this 'kenotic' (i.e. 'emptying') theory was based on Philippians 2:6–11, and in time became common. The stress in this scheme is still on the human figure.

3. The third scheme shifts the emphasis on to the prologue so that in effect it becomes Act 1. The pre-existent Christ was *God* from all eternity, who became man, and finally returned to his original glory. If Scheme 2 concentrates on an exalted

man, this concentrates on a thoroughly divine figure, a visitant who does not strip off his divinity as if it were clothing, but whose divinity remains 'in, with, and under' his humanity. Moreover, his pre-existence is not just as in Scheme 2 a projection backwards of what he became at his exaltation, but the key to the whole story. Naturally this was the scheme favoured by those who denied the real manhood of Jesus, the 'Docetists' for whom he only seemed to be a man. This view in that downright form has never been orthodox Christianity, but in practice it has probably been held by enormous numbers of Christians down the centuries, who have thought they were being orthodox.

The post-apostolic church inherited these patterns, and somehow had to reconcile them and produce a systematic doctrine. It *had to*, not really because earliest Christian tradition required it, for stories could have gone on being told without systematization. It had to rather because almost from the beginning the church has lived in a world where logic and consistency and coherence were important. Thus it rapidly became a body for which true doctrine was crucial, and for whom it was not enough simply to tell a story, or two or three stories. Indeed it may be that the story itself so focused attention on its central figure that questions about his nature were bound to arise if the story was to be understood.

Notes on Books

Jesus was a Real Man

J. D. G. Dunn, *Jesus and the Spirit*, SCM Press, 1975, Part I

R. E. Brown, *Jesus God and Man*, Geoffrey Chapman, 1968, ch. 2

J. A. T. Robinson, *The Human Face of God*, SCM Press, 1973, especially ch. 2

Contrary Evidence

R. E. Brown, *The Virginal Conception and Bodily Resurrection of Jesus*, Geoffrey Chapman, 1974, ch. 1 – a modern Roman Catholic account

Robinson as above, pp. 46ff on the virgin birth

Jesus as Sinless Man

G. W. H. Lampe, 'The Saving Work of Christ', in N. Pittenger (ed.), *Christ for Us Today*, SCM Press, 1968, pp. 141–153, especially pp. 143–5

C. F. D. Moule, 'The Manhood of Jesus in the New Testament', in S. W. Sykes and J. P. Clayton (eds.), *Christ, Faith and History*, Cambridge University Press, 1972, ch. 6

N. Pittenger, *Christology Reconsidered*, SCM Press, 1970, chs. 2 and 3

R. Williamson, 'Hebrews 4:15 and the Sinlessness of Jesus', *Expository Times* LXXXVI, 1 (October 1974), pp. 4–8

Robinson as above, pp. 88–98

Jesus as Corporate Man

C. F. D. Moule, *The Phenomenon of the New Testament*, SCM Press, 1967, ch. 2.

C. F. D. Moule, *The Origin of Christology*, Cambridge University Press, 1977, ch. 2

Patterns of Christology

J. Knox, *The Humanity and Divinity of Christ*, Cambridge University Press, 1967, ch. 1

III
The Question of Interpretation

7. Why not Chalcedon?

Rightly or wrongly, modern discussion about Jesus Christ often takes as a point of reference ancient formularies like the Nicene Creed and the Definition of Chalcedon. It must seem strange that we should now turn our attention away from 20th-century arguments to debates that took place in the 3rd, 4th, and 5th centuries, where even the names of the combatants are long since forgotten except by students and specialists. Yet out of these ancient debates came that Nicene Creed which is still recited by Christian congregations, and the Chalcedonian Definition which is still regarded by many as authoritative. Indeed many think these two formularies are still adequate expressions of Christian truth, though perhaps needing translation into more contemporary language. The Nicene Creed, which is notable chiefly for its solution to the problem of the relation of Christ to God, will be less our concern than the Definition, which deals particularly with who and what Jesus Christ is.

Why was there a Problem?

In the preceding pages we have seen that New Testament writers use both human and divine language about Jesus, and that there is not much attempt to systematize the differing descriptions of his nature and function. The New Testament does not go in for definitions, and indeed there were particular difficulties about proceeding to formulate any: the Jewish monotheistic roots of the church, watered by monotheistic strains from Hellenism, prevented Christians from proclaiming Christ as a second god, or as in some sense a fragment of God. At the same time it was strongly believed both that it was *God's* presence and salvation that was at work in Christ, for only one free from the taint of human sinfulness and weakness could rescue us, *and* that our salvation was from the inside, carried out by someone who was 'one of us'. 'What is not assumed cannot be restored,' said Gregory of Nazianzus (*Ep.* 101:7). A purely divine Christ was no more satisfactory than a purely human one.

But why did they need to clarify and systematize at all? Why try to express the inexpressible, why not tell two stories, one divine and one human, and live with the paradox? Why not sing hymns to Christ as to a god (which the Roman governor Pliny says the 2nd-century Christians did) but not try to define his divinity and humanity? Or, why could they not continue to speak in essentially *functional* terms, seeing Christ as the bearer of God's authority and power, as God's unique agent, without raising knotty problems about his nature? As a matter of fact, the second wave of Christian writings, the so-called Apostolic Fathers, in the main did just that, neither rationalizing nor systematizing their descriptions of Christ, but using both human and more-than-human language of him.

Significantly, it is with the 2nd-century 'Apologists' that we begin to find a more intellectual approach. As their name indicates, the Apologists' main aim was to defend and commend Christianity rationally before both Jews and Greeks. In practice this often meant arguing with philosophically-trained opponents, and to tell them a story or a pair of stories would simply not have worked. The Christian Apologists were obliged to fight with weapons of their adversaries' choosing, and that meant philosophical weapons, as we see as early as Justin Martyr. This was the first pressure towards systematization.

The second pressure came from within the Christians themselves. Increasingly they too had a Hellenistic and philosophical background, and naturally thought about their faith logically and systematically. They needed to get things clear, for their own sake as well as for apologetics. Given the intellectual climate, the outcome was inevitable.

The third pressure was the increasing need to set limits against heresy. On the one hand this meant safeguarding the genuine humanness of Jesus, and on the other it meant insisting that he was more than a Jewish messiah, more than the greatest of the prophets. The natural way of debating opposing dogmatic positions is intellectual and philosophical – and so we begin to define the indefinable.

The wish that the whole process of definition of doctrine had never begun is a romantic one. Given the time and the circumstances, what happened had to happen, and the attempt to define humanity and divinity in Christ in terms of 'substance' and 'nature' was a proper attempt. Yet it is true that the ways of thought of the early Christian centuries are not those of the New Testament, nor are they ours: the past really is different from the present, and its inhabitants had mental furniture different from ours. Anachronism is thus a constant danger, in two ways: first, it is too easy to read later solutions back into the New Testament, like assuming that 'Son of God' in Mark 1:1 refers to the Second Person of the Trinity; secondly, it is easy to forget that 4th- and 5th-century Christians did not necessarily mean what we mean by terms like 'substance', 'person', and 'nature'.

For good or ill, the intellectual process happened, and as far as Christ is concerned, two problems formed the foci of an ellipse. One was the trinitarian question, the question of how God could be one and indivisible if Jesus Christ is divine. The other was how he could be human, divine, and still one person. The two questions belong together, but at any given moment the debate tended to be about one *or* the other. Our concern is predominantly with the second, but it was the 'God-question' which first became acute, and was settled if not solved at the Council of Nicaea in 325, when it was laid down as orthodox that the one Lord Jesus Christ was

> the Son of God, begotten from the Father uniquely, that is of the substance of the Father, God from God, Light from Light, true God from true God, begotten not made, consubstantial (of one substance) with the Father ... who for us men and for our salvation came down and was made flesh, became man, suffered ...

Christ is God: 'of the substance of the Father' and 'consubstantial with the Father' put the point beyond doubt. He is God in no reduced or secondary sense, but in the same sense as the Father is. At the same time he really was man, not just God with a human body, though the creed gives more stress to the divinity. It was clear that the consequent question would have to be tackled: if all this is true, then what is Jesus Christ? Over a century later, the classical attempt to settle the question was made, but as the climax to nearly four centuries of debate in which Nicaea was only one stage, and during which there had been many solutions advanced, some simple, some complex. In going over some of these briefly now, we are not indulging antiquarian interests, but trying to see what is wrong with some of the apparently obvious solutions which have their attractions even now.

Simple Answers

1. Docetism. This ancient solution is also a very contemporary one, easily held by people who do not see its pitfalls. Docetism, or *Seemingism*, holds that while Jesus appeared to be a human being, he was really nothing of the kind. Underneath the appearance, he was God and not man. Some Docetists denied the reality of his human body, saying that he only seemed to eat, sleep, and die. Marcion, and most Gnostic Christians took this view. It comes in different forms, but all deny a real humanity usually because of two basic assumptions, neither grounded in the Jewish and Old Testament tradition, but both common in contemporary Hellenism.

The first assumption was that God is impassible, i.e. he cannot suffer change. Therefore Christ as God could not be born, grow, or die, but behind the appearance must be for ever eternally the same. The second assumption was that the physical world as a whole, and the human body in particular, are by their nature evil. God and the physical are as opposite as light and darkness, and therefore Christ could not have had a human body, for that would have made him part of the disease and not its cure.

The church officially never endorsed Docetism, usually

rejecting especially the second underlying assumption which was too closely associated with Gnosticism. There was too much in the gospels which ran counter to such Docetism, and in any case there was too strong a theological tradition (cf. Paul and Hebrews) which required a genuine humanity. Nevertheless it never stays away for long, and constitutes a perennial underground movement, sometimes strongest among those who are most jealous of their orthodoxy. This is not because of perversity, but it is a likely outcome of too strong and unqualified a stress on Christ's divinity. But how can we equate Jesus with God without removing him from mankind as usually understood?

2. *Ebionism* is the opposite way out of the dilemma. The Ebionites were probably the descendants of the earliest Jewish Christians, and held conservative views about the obligation of Christians to observe the Jewish Law, the Torah. They also held conservative views of Jesus, whom they recognized as messiah, but not as God. They did not proclaim only a human figure; J. Daniélou (*The Theology of Jewish Christianity*, chapter 7) has shown that they saw him as a superhuman being, and that those who favoured a purely human Jesus were few and out of touch with the main stream of thought. What was more common, and probably characteristic of the Ebionites, was 'adoptionism', according to which Jesus was raised to an exalted, divine status at some point – usually at the resurrection and/or exaltation, but sometimes at the baptism. This view fits much in the New Testament, though it cuts across passages which speak of pre-existence, but it does pre-suppose a second-grade divinity, not actually God, for one could scarely be promoted to divinity in the Old Testament sense! The model of God presupposed in adoptionism is either one in which a grade 2 god sits beside the original grade 1 God, or one in which the gap between man and the divine is in principle bridgeable. To repeat, what sort of divinity is it if someone can be promoted to it? All the same, adoptionism has a logic. It fits the twin facts that the Christ who was adored and worshipped had also

lived a human life, but as a solution its inadequacies were obvious, and it was not seriously entertained in any widespread way.

3. A divine mind/soul in a human body is also a simple and obvious solution. It posits a Jesus with a human body like ours in every way (except perhaps for its virginal conception, which would not however raise the genetic difficulties for the ancient world that it does for us). It also posits for Jesus not a human centre of consciousness but a divine one, namely the eternal Logos of God. The whole person Jesus Christ was formed by the union of the Logos not with the fullness of human nature, but with *flesh*, i.e. with a human body. Instead of two persons, one human and one divine, there is only the divine person, the humanity being strictly impersonal and confined to the physical. The Logos takes the place of the human mind or soul, and infuses the divine energy into the whole person, and the unity of Jesus is no more imperilled by this than by the union of mind and body in anyone else, according to the contemporary view of man. In the history of doctrine this sort of view is known as the heresy of Apollinarius, and eventually was firmly rejected by the church. Yet many people in ancient and modern times have held a similar view, and to picture Jesus as essentially God in a human body seems such a simple and sensible solution that it is fair to ask why it should be judged heretical.

There are two reasons. First, the Jesus of the gospels has a human mind: he can be ignorant and mistaken, and there are things he cannot do, despite his sense of communion with God. Secondly, and probably of more importance, whatever God-in-a-human-body could be called, he could never be called a genuinely human being. What does not have a human mind is not human. As a footnote we can add a modern objection that this solution depends on a view of man as divisible into parts which was common at the time, but fits neither the biblical nor the modern understanding of man.

None of the simple 'solutions' solved the problem.

Complex Answers

These did not follow the simple answers chronologically. The whole debate had far less structure and progression than our present outline may suggest. We are merely trying to gain a broad picture of the struggles and arguments of three or four centuries.

1. A stress on the complete Godhead and the complete manhood of Jesus was characteristic of the theologians of Antioch. It reached its peak in what was unjustly alleged to be the view of Nestorius that there were in effect 'two Sons' in Christ, two individuals, but was perhaps an attempt to live with the paradox of a Jesus who was fully human, in mind as in body, but also fully God, and no mere expression of the divine. Passages like Romans 1:3f, 8 could be cited in support of the view, which indeed fitted a good deal of the New Testament, but which never solved the problem of how to talk convincingly about Jesus as one person. Despite the accusations of their detractors, the Antiochene theologians did continually maintain their acceptance of the fact that he was, mysteriously, one person, but it did undoubtedly often sound as if they really had in mind a pair of beings somehow yoked together. Their intention was to safeguard the true humanity of Jesus which they believed to be threatened, but their account failed to be plausible. How did the two persons relate to one another? Who was responsible for which action? Did the two wills alternate in operation? Was it the human person who prayed, and the divine who forgave sins? The questions are endless and the answers either unsatisfactory or lacking altogether, but the great unanswered question was how they could refer to Jesus Christ in the singular.

Yet this scheme did take the humanity seriously. There was no talk of the odd notion of an impersonal humanity, and the divine Logos was seen as united with a whole man, not just with a human body. Indeed its proponents affirmed without reserve the oneness of Christ, but the trouble was that they never found a satisfying logical way of explaining it.

101

2. To stress the oneness of Jesus Christ into which the human and the divine must somehow fit, is to start from the other end of the conundrum, and is what the Alexandrian theologians did. They began with the divine as well as with the unity, and argued that the Logos became truly man (human mind as well as human body), but somehow without a second (human) centre of consciousness. This was to risk sliding into Apollinarianism and to see Jesus as God-in-a-human-body, but at their best the Alexandrians avoided the trap and taught a truly human Christ. They saw the human and divine natures as related in much the same way as the soul and body in any ordinary human being who is of course still one individual (this was known technically to the history of doctrine as the *hypostatic* union). Moreover, the unity was confirmed by the 'interchange of properties' (*communicatio idiomatum*) between the divine and human natures respectively, and the one person. This was a way of saying that the one Jesus Christ shares all the human and the divine properties, without the 'natures' that provide those properties being in any way confused or mixed with one another.

Inevitably however, because divinity is infinitely more powerful than humanity, it tended in Alexandrian thought to swamp the human nature. In practice, though deference was paid to the importance of the human, Christ was thought of as a divine figure. He was one, and he was divine (and human, but that tended to be less emphasized). Indeed, in the 5th century and up to the present day, some heirs of the Alexandrian position have argued that whatever was true of the two natures before the incarnation, after it there was only one, and that divine (the heresy of Eutyches), while others have argued that there was only one *will*, and that divine. At all events, Alexandrian thinking has not always been totally convincing in its endorsement of the humanness of Jesus.

Footnote
There was another kind of solution altogether, one that goes back to Origen, and was defended by the arch-heretic Arius. This sees Christ's divinity as in some way secondary to God's,

102

as derived and subordinate. Such a notion was rejected at Nicaea in the struggle about the nature of God, and was not helpful in later controversies. It is what it implies about God that is unsatisfactory, and its introduction of a third entity between divinity and humanity. Similar objections to those made against adoptionism apply here, and in any case the question of divine and human in one person, Christ, still remains.

The Chalcedonian Solution

Chalcedon took for granted what had been decided at Nicaea, namely that Christ was true God of true God, of one substance with the Father (i.e. divine in the same sense that God is divine). It attempted, not so much to solve the problem of the relation of divine to human in Christ, as to define the limits within which a solution must be found. It implicitly excluded some extreme positions, including extremes of both the Antiochene and Alexandrian parties. Despite its at first sight stupefying language, the Definition is crucial.

> We all agree in teaching men to acknowledge one and the same Son, our Lord Jesus Christ, at once complete in Godhead and complete in manhood, truly God and truly man, consisting also of a rational soul and body; of one substance with the Father as regards his Godhead, and at the same time of one substance with us as regards his manhood; like us in all respects, except for sin; as regards his Godhead, begotten of the Father before the ages, but yet as regards his manhood begotten ... of the Virgin Mary, the God-bearer; one and the same Christ, Son, Lord, Only-begotten, recognized in two natures, without confusion, without change, without division, without separation; the distinction of natures being in no way removed by the union, but rather the characteristics of each nature being preserved and coming together to form one person and subsistence, not as though he were parted or divided into two persons, but one and the same Son and Only-begotten God the Word, Lord Jesus Christ ...

Why do we bother today with such doublespeak? Because this tortuous piece has been the reference point of discussion ever since, and is still of authority today for large sections of the Christian world. For a proper unpacking of the Definition one must go to books about it, like that of Sellers, or to histories of Christian thought, like those of Grillmeier and Kelly. For our modest purposes, we can at least note that it is trying to safeguard three things, all of which had been threatened.

    1. Jesus is divine, in the full and not any reduced sense.

    2. Jesus is human in every way (except that he is free from sin).

    3. Jesus is one person, not a divine-human partnership.

Nothing very new is said, but boundaries are set. To a degree, the debate had been concerned with forging verbal tools, so that 'person' and 'subsistence' (*hypostasis*) came to refer to the concrete individual, and 'nature' (*phusis*) for the divinity and humanity which are joined in the one person yet remain distinct. How technically we should take these words is disputed. It is possible to say (with Bernard Lonergan, *A Second Collection*, p. 259) that 'person' is what there are three of in the trinity and one of in Christ, and 'nature' is what there is one of in the trinity and two of in Christ, and that we are bound to Chalcedon's metaphysics no further than this.

Whether or not its metaphysics is binding, the Definition's purport is authoritative for the Roman Catholic Church, and Article 2 of the Anglican 39 Articles is based on it. The Church of England's 1922 *Report on Doctrine* asserts the same truths as Chalcedon. Yet the Definition is now under serious question in some quarters not only because of the obsolete conceptions in which it is framed, but even for what it is trying to say through those conceptions. Its original purpose was to reconcile into one acceptable statement the viewpoints of Antioch and Alexandria, taking the truths from each and eliminating possible sources of error at the same time. If it is now being attacked, how successful was it in its own day, and what is wrong with it now?

Criticisms of the Definition

1. It did not work. It did not effect reconciliation, but itself became a centre of protest, and those for example who had believed in only one nature of Christ after the incarnation, went on believing that.

2. Its highly abstract character tends to obscure the concrete historical Jesus of Nazareth who ate and slept and died. Its unintended effect is to encourage Docetism, for Christ tends to become a theological conundrum involving natures and persons, and not an individual at all.

3. For moderns, its conceptual tools are unhelpful. The notion of something called humanity and something called divinity, both with properties which must be related without being confused or separated, is uncongenial or even meaningless now. At the time of Chalcedon people may have believed in the real existence of abstractions like humanity and divinity, but to us they are merely convenient generalizations. We do not believe in a thing called humanity of which there may be more or less, which can combine with other things, and we certainly do not find it natural to speak of humanity and divinity as *substances* in any sense whatsoever.

4. The doctrines of both man and God presupposed by the Definition are unsatisfactory. No doubt unintentionally, it tends to give the impression that divinity and humanity are commensurate entities that must be fitted together somehow; in fact, they are not comparable entities at all, for God is the one who sustains and enables all things, including all people, to be what they are. If we must speak abstractly, all humanity is dependent on divinity, and the two are of different orders.

5. In their day, formularies like the Definition may well have said what was appropriate and necessary, but when they become ossified as standards of orthodoxy for centuries, they are dangerous. Even if we wish to say the same things as the Chalcedonian Fathers, we must use our own words and conceptions, not theirs. Ought we to become 5th-century people when we work at christology?

6. All talk of God is by its nature likely to leave the mind

105

reeling, but the Definition overcomes us with confusion, not with awe and mystery.

In the history of Christian thought, the 'heretics' seem always to have had the clear, simple solutions, and the 'orthodox' a monopoly of obscurity. Indeed orthodoxy seems in a state of unstable equilibrium, always in danger of tilting over into one heresy or another. One reason for this is that clarity of thought was not the only consideration; it was also important that doctrine should express what Christians did in prayer and worship, and this sometimes outran more cautious rational approaches. But what are we to do with this sort of definition of belief about Christ? Ignore it, translate it into our terms, re-express its basic intentions, or take it as it stands? We are due back in the 20th century!

Notes on Books

Generally useful on the history of the debates
> A. Grillmeier, *Christ in Christian Tradition*, A. R. Mowbray, 2nd edn., 1975
>
> J. M. Creed, *The Divinity of Jesus Christ*, Collins/Fontana, 1964
>
> J. N. D. Kelly, *Early Christian Doctrines*, A. & C. Black, 1958
>
> T. E. Pollard, *Johannine Christology and the Early Church*, Cambridge University Press, 1970 – especially useful for the build-up to Nicaea
>
> M. F. Wiles, *The Making of Christian Doctrine*, Cambridge University Press, 1967, chs. 3, 4, and 5
>
> M. F. Wiles, 'The Doctrine of Christ in the Patristic Age', in N. Pittenger (ed.), *Christ for Us Today*, SCM Press, 1968, ch. 5

Specifically on Chalcedon
> J. McIntyre, *The Shape of Christology*, SCM Press, 1964, ch. 4
>
> P. Schoonenberg, *The Christ*, Sheed & Ward, 1972, pp. 51–66
>
> R. V. Sellers, *The Council of Chalcedon*, SPCK, 1953

Also

J. Daniélou, *The Theology of Jewish Christianity*, Darton, Longman & Todd, 1964, ch. 7

W. F. J. Ryan and B. J. Tyrrell (eds.), *A Second Collection: Papers by Bernard J. F. Lonergan*, Darton, Longman & Todd and Herder, New York, 1974

8. Myth or Truth?

However odd it may be to modern ears, the Definition of Chalcedon and the Nicene Creed were attempts to take full account of Jesus Christ. The New Testament is often ambiguous, and provides no systematic picture of him, but the ancient formularies provide a framework in which the loose ends can be brought together. The question now is how far their answers are satisfactory for 20th-century questions, and even how far the New Testament statements can still be taken at their face value.

The Myth of God Incarnate

In 1977 England saw a minor theological rumpus when a group of theologians published under the editorship of John Hick a symposium with the provocative title *The Myth of God Incarnate* (referred to as *Myth*). It quickly went through several impressions, and gained for its contributors some admiration and gratitude, some scholarly criticism, and quite a lot of vulgar abuse. Some people burst into print on the subject without having understood the issues, and to a degree this was the fault of the book itself. It suffered, like all symposia, from the fact that while its contributors were heading in roughly the same direction, they were taking somewhat different routes to not precisely the same destination. It is not easy to talk about the book as a whole. The title did not help: 'myth' is a confusing word, and was undoubtedly taken to mean 'untrue', so that the book was taken to say simply that Jesus was not God incarnate.

In fact what appears to unite the mixed bunch of scholars is that they find the language and conception of 'incarnation' difficult and no longer appropriate. 'Incarnation' on Maurice Wiles's definition (p. 1) is the doctrine that Jesus Christ is both fully divine and fully human, yet one person – the doctrine whose emergence to definition we have just been sketching. This is called 'myth' in the technical sense that it is a way of expressing something by means of a story, a story about heavenly and divine realities, put in human terms. A myth may or may not be true, in this use of the word, but it is certainly not *literally* true (Wiles, *Myth*, p. 165). Applied to the incarnation, it refers to the story of God's sending his Son to become man. This is myth because God does not literally have a Son, nor were there two divine individuals one of whom sent the other off to visit another place and to become a human being. It is anthropomorphism in story form, using human activity as a model for, a way of talking about, divine activity, and therefore at best an approximation. It cannot be taken literally, for God's becoming man cannot be taken literally – manhood is not a quality that can be added or subtracted like kindness or blondness or shortness. Being a man is what one is, and God cannot just add manhood to his qualities, unless he ceases to be God, which he could scarcely do! No, this is picture language, myth, and is not to be taken at its face value, even though for the most part we may use it happily and unreflectingly.

According to *Myth*, what happened was something like this. Granted that Jesus Christ was or became crucial to his followers, and granted that in his life, mission, death and resurrection they saw a decisive revelation of God, it was natural in their intellectual environment that the idea of his divinity should emerge (though Frances Young, *Myth* pp. 118f, shows that really close contemporary analogies are lacking). The belief in an incarnation grew stronger and more precise over four or five centuries, and was the way in which early Christians expressed the significance of Jesus for them. It is not, however, a natural way for us to express his significance for us, but happily it is possible to have a genuine Christian faith without it. We must get behind the myth and ask how we in our 20th-century words and conceptions can convey what the doctrine of the incarnation conveyed in the 3rd, 4th, and 5th centuries. It is not a matter of putting the

Chalcedonian Definition or the Nicene Creed in modern dress, but of getting at the fundamental intentions behind them, and putting those intentions in modern conceptions and modern words. The doctrine of the God-man, the incarnation, is like a nut which can be cracked to get at the kernel. The job of interpretation is first to do the cracking, and then to devise a new unmythological housing for the kernel.

Little said in *Myth* was new, and its basic position was already well conveyed in the writings of some of the contributors, notably Maurice Wiles in *The Remaking of Christian Doctrine* (1974) and in a number of important articles. Nevertheless it came as a shock to many people, who welcomed with relief the replies that appeared with startling speed.

The Truth of God Incarnate

George Carey produced a courteous small book (*God Incarnate*, 1977) which concentrated on those biblical passages which emphasize the more-than-human role and nature of Christ, and he re-asserted traditional evangelical doctrine without really grappling with the difficulties that lead the *Myth* symposiasts to take the view they do. E. L. Mascall in *Theology and the Gospel of Christ* (1978) has a chapter in which he castigates *Myth* and its position. Most well-known, however, was a book which included contributions from evangelical and catholic camps, *The Truth of God Incarnate* (1977) (referred to as *Truth*), edited by Michael Green who was also the major contributor. Its title conveys the book's condemnation of the implications of the title of *Myth*. *Truth* was no more of a unified position than its target, and there are one or two glaring lapses of courtesy in it, but its chief defect is that it does not make clear the underlying issues. This is a pity, for it and *Myth* do stand – at times a little incoherently – for two basically different approaches to the question of Christ, and indeed to the questions of the being of God and of religious language. Rather than working through the arguments of these books, and certainly rather than trying to

110

assess their respective merits, we shall try to examine these fundamental differences.

Briefly, it may be said that *Truth* is content with a Chalcedonian position, and holds that it is better to revise our 20th-century preconceptions than to tailor our beliefs to fit them. God sent his Son to become man: the Bible teaches it, and the early church defined its meaning. This is saving truth, and though of course there are difficulties in understanding it, we cannot consider changing the basic statement. Probably not all the contributors would agree on how important the precise solution of Chalcedon is, but they are united in wanting to say that Christ is God, and man, and yet one. What are their reasons?

First there is religious experience as interpreted by Christian tradition. Experience of Christ is God-experience, and for its validation requires that Christ be God. Deny this, then Christ-experience may perhaps not be God-experience, and we are adrift on a sea of uncertainty. Secondly, the New Testament supports the view that Christ is God, man, and one. Green spends a good deal of time arguing this (chapter 1), and he in particular believes that the abandonment of a conservative view of biblical inspiration is the cause of a good deal of trouble (chapter 6). Get rid of excessive historical scepticism, and you begin to restore belief in the deity of Jesus Christ. Thirdly, at least in Michael Green's case, the biblical picture of an active personal God is accepted as accurate; God really does act in just the way described (e.g. pp. 10, 12).

Both sides, I think, agree that there is a problem, but disagree about how serious it is. We shall try now to elucidate the matter first by looking at a couple of problem areas, and then by looking at the underlying divergences.

The Virgin Birth
When we discussed this in chapter 6, we noted that for some modern Christians the stories of a virginal conception that are to be found in the early chapters of Matthew and Luke (and only there) are a pictorial, 'mythical' way of establishing the

belief that behind the ordinary human life of Jesus, we have nothing less than the initiative of God. The story is not literally true, but it does give the key theological insight that God is crucially at work in this man. It is an example of how something can be true on one level, the theological, even if found not to be true on another, the biological. This, needless to say, is the view virtually taken for granted in *Myth* (see pp. 2f, 7, 80, 106). It is a way of conveying the significance of the birth of Jesus.

The other view, held at least by Michael Green in *Truth* (pp. 10, 12, 37f, 40f), is that while the theological significance is strongly affirmed, so is the biological basis. Jesus really was born of a female ovum that had not been fertilized by a male sperm. All sorts of arguments are used on both sides, and the similarities with and differences from stories about miraculous births in Jewish and pagan traditions are examined (the best recent account of the whole topic is in R. E. Brown, *The Virginal Conception and Bodily Resurrection of Jesus*, chapter 1), but I suspect that behind the immediate question lies a tacit disagreement about how God works in the world. If he is believed to work primarily or even exclusively in and through natural processes, then probably Jesus will be thought to have had his biological origin from two human parents, with the virginal conception story giving the significance of the event. If, on the other hand, God is believed to work at least sometimes *across* the natural processes, then the story of a virginal conception is more likely to be taken literally as a biological and not just a theological statement.

The Pre-existence of Christ

We saw in chapter 5 that the notion of the personal pre-existence of Christ does occur in the New Testament, though scarcely a common motif. Incarnation presupposes pre-existence: God sends his already-existing Son to become man, and finally to return whence he came. The contemporary problem with the whole idea is that it is hard to see how such a divine visitor could be human.

We have seen some of the ancient attempts to deal with the

112

problem. Another, that has been sporadically canvassed in the last century and a half is the 'kenotic' (i.e. 'emptying') theory, according to which the divine Son voluntarily stripped himself of some of his divine attributes, such as omnipotence, omnipresence, and omniscience, and received them back after his resurrection and exaltation. This theory still has its attractions, but few scholars now propose it, if only because divine attributes are not things that can be added or subtracted like bits of clothing but are part of the definition of deity, they are what make God to be God (see Don Cupitt in *Myth*, p. 137; and D. M. Baillie in *God Was in Christ*, pp.94–8, for criticisms which have been decisive for many English-speaking readers, though the latter were written back in 1948). If the distinctively divine things are removed, in what sense is the resulting being still divine?

Even the kenotic theory does not solve the problem of the oneness of God which accompanies the problem of the humanness of Jesus. If Christ is personally pre-existent, how can God be one? The traditional answer is that the personal pre-existence of God the Son does not mean the individual pre-existence of Jesus Christ. This sounds meaningless but in fact the distinction is important, and can claim support from the Chalcedonian Definition. What is pre-existent is the *divine* in Christ, not the human nor the incarnate Christ. This solution of course rests upon the two-natures theory of Christ – one of the natures is pre-existent and the other is not.

The *Myth* way of taking pre-existence, shared by many people, avoids such complications altogether. It exploits the fact we have already noted that in Judaism, to ascribe pre-existence to something is to ascribe fundamental or even ultimate significance to it, as in the cases of the Torah, the Temple, the Sabbath, and the person of Moses. It was part of God's primal purpose and existed in his intention from all eternity. So, in the case of Christ, we do not mean that the individual Jesus Christ existed before he was born, but that *what God was in Christ he had always been*. Some writers, like John Robinson (in *The Human Face of God*, pp. 151–179), think that the New Testament writers themselves were deliberately being 'metaphorical' in talking of Christ's pre-existence, and really meant the sort of thing we have just been saying. Others, like Anthony Hanson (in *Grace and Truth*, pp. 67ff), think that some New Testament writers did believe in his literal, personal pre-existence. For us, whatever the New Testament writers themselves believed, this must be interpreted to mean that God has not changed his nature or his purpose, but has always in principle been the God and Father of our Lord Jesus Christ, the God whom Christians find present and active in the human life of Jesus.

One reason for such an interpretation is that the alternative is taken to be a Christ who is not fully human but a divine visitor in human dress. Yet behind this is a more basic disagreement about how to talk appropriately about God and about his nature. Our two examples, the virginal conception and the pre-existence, are pointers to this important underlying issue.

Religious Language

It is hard to avoid the conclusion that behind the differences between the *Myth* and *Truth* approaches lies a difference about the nature and status of religious language. Take 'Jesus is the Son of God'. As we saw in chapter 5, this is not straightforward language, for God does not have a wife and does not father children. Moreover, in ordinary speech, 'father and son' requires two related but quite distinctive individuals, but Christian orthodoxy requires no such thing! In terms that go back to Thomas Aquinas, 'Father–Son' is *analogical* language; in Ian Ramsey's terms, it is a *model*. Analogical language is not straightforward. God is not a Father in exactly the same sense as a human father, nor is Jesus his Son in precisely the human sense. Yet analogical language is not merely metaphorical either, for 'Jesus is the Son of God' is not just like 'Jesus is the door of the sheepfold', which is clearly metaphorical. The connection in the Father–Son case is much closer than that because human

114

father-son relationships are reflections of the divine Father–Son relationship, because man is created by God. One is an analogy of the other.

We cannot talk straightforwardly about God precisely because God is not just one more item in the universe, along with ships, shoes, sealing-wax, cabbages, and kings. God on the contrary is the explanation of them all and of all that is, and even of me as I try to talk about him – so I talk analogically or use models. Similarly, I cannot talk directly about electricity because I have no direct experience of what it is, so instead I use the model of a stream and talk about 'current'. I cannot talk about molecules directly, so I use bonding diagrams. I cannot talk directly about God's inner life, so I use the model of the Father–Son relationship. We use models, or talk analogically, not because we choose to, but because 'the only alternative is silence' as Augustine once pointed out (*De Trinitate* V ix 10). The examples just used show that analogical talking is not peculiar to God-talk, but it is particularly important and necessary there, and this is accepted on all sides. Its very oddity is a sign that something out of the ordinary is being attempted.

When we come to the incarnation, part of our difficulty is that some of the language is analogical and some is not. 'Jesus went about doing good' seems straightforward. 'The Word became flesh' is certainly not. In talking about Christ we easily slide from one sort of language to another, and may even forget that there are two sorts involved or tacitly assume there is only one sort.

Conservatives generally, including some of the *Truth* contributors, seem to assume that the incarnation is revealed truth, and that in so far as analogies are involved, *the analogies are part of the revelation*. If you try to unpack the language as the *Myth* people do, you are not cracking a nut, you are peeling an onion. There is no kernel, but like an onion the various layers are the thing itself, and not expendable. This is perhaps why Michael Green, and even E. L. Mascall, never seem to close with the problems that concern *Myth*'s contributors and people like them, but do rather a lot of rebuking and rather a lot of restating the traditional and orthodox point of view. The problem is not *felt*.

On the other side, whatever label we give them, are people for whom what is expressed in analogy or model language can and must now be put in some other way. The model or analogy is not part of the given or of the revelation, but of its communication. The knock-down question, 'Is Jesus or is he not the Son of God?' is strictly unanswerable, because to unpack such language and discover what is meant by it is what the game is all about. Much controversy between the two positions seems to be through a mist of mutual incomprehension. Some of the *Truth* people, notably Green, seem to find *Myth* perverse, but equally the *Myth* people and others like them give little overt attention to the possibility that they are dealing with an onion rather than a nut. Yet it is at least conceivable that what Maurice Wiles and others want to do cannot be done, that the only way of saying what the incarnation means is in incarnation language, and that there is no kernel which can be detached from its casing and rehoused.

Our basic question is whether traditional statements about Jesus Christ as the God-man can still be taken as they stand, or whether they must and can be re-expressed in more acceptable modern terms. However it is not just a matter of religious language, it is also a matter of the sort of God we are talking about: can we reasonably speak of a God who becomes man and visits this earth?

The Nature of God

Michael Green (*Truth* pp. 10, 12, 112f) explicitly adopts the viewpoint apparently assumed in the Bible that God is to be seen in intervention terms, active in a thoroughly personal way, and to be found particularly in the extraordinary, unusual, and humanly inexplicable. One meets this God when he answers a prayer, when human resources fail and God steps in, when miracle occurs, and in religion – in reading the Bible, in prayer, and in worship. Of course he is not just a magnified human being, but he can be spoken of in human

116

categories without undue distortion. In the incarnation it is natural to speak of his *coming* amongst men and women, and equally natural to cope with problems of relating two *persons*, one human and one divine, in one individual. God is relatively easy to talk to, and even talk about. The drawback is that we tend to fit him into the gaps left by ordinary events and circumstances, and this can sometimes seem anthropomorphic to the point of incredibility.

The other view is really a different emphasis rather than a different doctrine. We saw in the case of the virginal conception that it came down to how God is believed characteristically to work in the world, through or across the natural processes. The 'through the natural processes' emphasis implies a God who is not only the first cause of everything, but even now sustains all that is, is the ground of all being. He is the explanation of everything not only as the starting-point, but as the present enabler. It is a little like a painting: we see everything but the canvas which is altogether implicit and not explicit at all, yet without it there would be no painting. Similarly God is to be detected – rather than seen – especially in the ordinary. He is the implicit rather than the explicit God, who is present in, with, and under all that is, which is partly why we can speak of him only analogically and in strange uses of language. When this God acts in the world, he acts not across but through ordinary things and ordinary people, and not across ordinary causality but through it.

If the danger of the first God is that he can be too exclusively a God of the gaps, the danger of this one is that he can be absorbed without remainder into the world as a sort of pantheistic presence or impersonal force, though its protagonists no more intend this than the protagonists of the other view intend a God of the gaps. When all is said about holding a balance between a God who works implicitly and one who works explicitly, and about both pictures holding some of the truth, the difference between these two emphases is crucial. Of course they are not at all points incompatible, but they are different enough to lead to different styles of piety, different understandings of the miraculous, of the

117

world, of religion, and of how Christ should be interpreted. Although they may inhabit the same church or congregation, those who hold these differing views at times seem almost to inhabit different worlds.

Nevertheless, the proponents of an implicit God may well agree that the life and ministry of Jesus Christ constitutes an event in which the presence and activity of God may be detected unusually clearly, and that it is the key to a great deal else, a moment of critical and even final disclosure. It is by this event that other events are interpreted, and by this man that we know God to be at work where he cannot be so easily discerned. Yet this is not to deny the ambiguity in this as in all other places of revelation, for even here it is through and not across the human that God acts. *How* God may be regarded as acting in Christ if we adopt this 'implicit' view will be the subject of our final chapter.

Notes on Books

The Myth of God Incarnate
> J. Hick (ed.), *The Myth of God Incarnate*, SCM Press, 1977
> M. F. Wiles, *The Remaking of Christian Doctrine*, SCM Press, 1974

The Truth of God Incarnate
> G. Carey, *God Incarnate*, Inter-Varsity Press, 1977
> M. Green (ed.), *The Truth of God Incarnate*, Hodder & Stoughton, 1977
> B. L. Hebblethwaite, 'The Appeal to Experience in Christology', in S. W. Sykes and J. P. Clayton (eds.), *Christ, Faith and History*, Cambridge University Press, 1972, ch.15
> E. L. Mascall, *Theology and the Gospel of Christ*, SPCK, 1978

The Virgin Birth
> R. E. Brown, *The Virginal Conception and Bodily Resurrection of Jesus*, Geoffrey Chapman, 1974, ch.1
> *Myth* and *Truth* as above

The Pre-existence of Christ

D. M. Baillie, *God Was in Christ*, Faber & Faber, 1948, pp. 94–8 on kenoticism

G. B. Caird, 'The Development of the Doctrine of Christ in the New Testament', in N. Pittenger (ed.), *Christ for Us Today*, SCM Press, 1968, pp. 66–80

A. T. Hanson, *Grace and Truth*, SPCK, 1975, ch. 4

J. Knox, *The Humanity and Divinity of Christ*, Cambridge University Press, 1967, chs. 4 and 6

J. A. T. Robinson, *The Human Face of God*, SCM Press, 1973, pp. 143–179

P. Schoonenberg, *The Christ*, Sheed & Ward, 1972, pp. 80–91

Myth as above

Religious Language

J. Macquarrie, *God-Talk*, SCM Press, 1967

E. L. Mascall, *Words and Images*, Longmans Green & Co., 1957

E. L. Mascall, *Theology and Images*, A. R. Mowbray, 1963

H. Palmer, *Analogy*, Macmillan, 1973 – an excellent introduction,with most of the relevant passages from Aquinas printed in an appendix

I. T. Ramsey, *Models and Mystery*, Oxford University Press, 1964

I. T. Ramsey, *Religious Language*, SCM Press, 1967

The Nature of God

N. Pittenger, *Christology Reconsidered*, SCM Press, 1970, pp. 135–146

Truth and Schoonenberg as above

9. Solutions?

Many people have simply given up trying to make sense of what is traditionally said by Christians about Jesus, and instead they regard him as one of the very greatest human beings of all time. I have not tried to explore this point of view. There are many on the other hand who are content with the kind of belief proclaimed at Chalcedon (Christ is God, Christ is man, Christ is one), and while agreeing that there are enormous difficulties in understanding it, accept those difficulties as unavoidable. There are still others, who consider themselves to be firmly within the Christian camp, and who wish to say more-than-human things about Jesus Christ, who none the less fully accept modern psychological and sociological insights into what it is to be human, and for whom the 'two-natures' approach to the understanding of Christ no longer works. Yet they cannot just drop the whole matter, but look for other ways to say what they believe ought to be said. As Maurice Wiles has often said, our need is not to translate what our forefathers said, but to find ways in our words and conceptions to fulfil the same intentions that they fulfilled in their words and conceptions.

In this chapter, we shall look at a highly selective handful of suggestions that have been made to do just that. At the end of *Truth*, John Macquarrie fairly points out that *Myth* attacks a version of incarnation-belief which is basically that of the divine visitor, with its consequent problems for the genuine humanity of Jesus. Indeed some of his fellow-contributors to *Truth* seem to have fallen into the trap of accepting and defending such a view. There are hints from B. C. Butler (chapter 4), but it is with Macquarrie's brief postscript that *Myth* is explicitly taken to task for ignoring the modern restatements of the incarnation which try to overcome the problems which *Myth* quite properly highlights. Thus, for example, John Robinson's important *The Human Face of God* (first published in 1973, and having a fourth impression in 1977, the year of *Myth*), is mentioned only by Frances Young (*Myth*, p. 47). Schoonenberg is not mentioned at all, though *The Christ* appeared in English in 1972.

In what follows I shall give the sketchiest of introductions to some interesting and important modern attempts to fulfil the intention of Chalcedon, and indeed of the varied New Testament witness, without using obsolete words or conceptions. At this point it must be stressed that it is quite impossible to fit these new suggestions into old frameworks, though this is what their critics often try to do. Some of the theologians we shall mention believe themselves to be faithfully conveying what Chalcedon conveyed, some are consciously setting themselves against it, and some may not be interested either way, but all are trying to do something new and to use a new framework of one sort or another. Some highly important thinkers I do not discuss at all, such as Barth, Bonhoeffer, Kasper, Lonergan, Rahner, and Tillich. I ignore important theories, and even those that are mentioned are not treated in detail nor subjected to serious criticism. Moreover, I must emphasize that my aim is not to provide my own solution to the question about Jesus as both man and God, but rather to illustrate some of the solutions at present on offer, in the hope that readers may be prompted to consider seriously their own responses.

Chalcedon Re-stated

As we saw in the last chapter, one serious option is to re-affirm Chalcedonian christology, with due explanation and inter-pretation, and to expound two natures in one person. There are sophisticated and influential theologians who do this, such as E. L. Mascall who in a series of books, most recently in *Theology and the Gospel of Christ* (1978), has rejected what he regards as attempts to tailor Christian theology to fit the spirit and preconceptions of the 20th-century western world. He also rejects all attempts to by-pass the ancient formularies, and considers that Chalcedon and its notions of 'substance' and 'nature' remains inescapably the basis for christology.

No one knows better than Mascall that religious language uses images, for he has written several books on the subject, and he does not suppose that we can talk about God or the incarnation without using analogy, but he is among those who consider that the images, analogies, and even presumably what is often called 'myth', *are themselves part of the revelation*. This is implicit in much of his writing, but is explicit in *Words and Images* (pp. 109–126) and in *Theology and Images* (pp. 42ff). Thus notions like incarnation are of the sort that participate in the reality of what they represent, and are therefore not alterable or expendable, despite what some theologians suppose. Instead of theology putting what it has to say in the words and conceptions of contemporary thought, it may need to teach the modern world a new (though old) language.

This comes out sharply in Mascall's review of *God as Spirit* by G. W. H. Lampe (*Journal of Theological Studies*, October 1978, pp. 617–621), in which he accuses Lampe of unitarianism and adoptionism. The first charge may be fair enough, but the second reveals just how far apart he and Lampe are. As we shall see below, Lampe is proposing a whole new conceptual framework within which to deal with major questions of theology, including christology, and the word 'adoptionism' has no meaning within that framework. Mascall does not consider a new conceptual framework to be possible or permissible, and fears that biblical faith cannot survive if forced into what he sees as a logically inappropriate structure. He must therefore judge Lampe's work in his own traditional terms, and not surprisingly condemns it.

Mascall knows that simply to re-affirm the traditional two-natures doctrine is not enough and that it must be explained and defended. It must be confessed that like many such defenders, he is easiest to follow when attacking those who (in his view) wrongly compromise with modern thought, and hardest when commending the ancient truths. Rather aston-

122

ishingly he will not accept that the spirit of our times makes it any harder to believe in, say, the pre-existence of Christ, than did the spirit of the 5th century. Christ, he maintains, was both divine and human, and his life was lived on two levels at the same time, but this must not be reduced to saying that there are two stories (one divine and one human) told about the same events. The greatest difficulty he has is in presenting us with a convincingly human Jesus, and this is true also of Norman Anderson's *The Mystery of the Incarnation* (1978), and indeed of many defences of the divinity of Christ.

We turn now to attempts to by-pass the whole conundrum by using approaches quite different from the two-nature model of Chalcedon and after.

Event not Person

The American scholar John Knox holds that it is unfruitful to talk of 'natures' and 'persons', and that instead we should speak of 'events' and 'functions', because whatever may have been possible for ancient man, we cannot believe in a real human being who was pre-existent. If Christ was pre-existent, he was not a true human being, for his identity was not formed as part of the living stream of mankind and in particular as the genetic product of a father and a mother. Moreover, if we talk in terms of pre-existence only of Christ in so far as he was divine, we must also talk about divine and human 'natures' in him, which leads to the problem of how one individual can have two natures. He thinks we need a different model, the model not of divine being but of divine activity (see especially *The Humanity and Divinity of Christ*, 1967). God was in Christ, but actively not statically, as 2 Corinthians 5:19 does in fact go on to say. God *acted* in Christ, but this did not entail some kind of non-human nature in him. Christ revealed God, acted as God's agent, and in Christ's words and actions we encounter God, but the words and actions are those of a human being. Knox does not adhere to the view that only the divine can reveal the divine, for God acts through the *human* person of Christ.

He can claim substantial New Testament support for his view. Even Oscar Cullmann in his *The Christology of the New Testament* shows throughout that we are dealing with functional rather than ontological christology, i.e. with functions, events and actions rather than natures. His way of putting the point is to say that all christology is *Heilsgeschichte*, the story of God's saving activity. Moreover, to concentrate on function and action rather than natures is arguably a very Hebraic and biblical thing to do; it is only when the reflective (Hellenistic ?) mind gets to work that we start thinking about the nature of Christ, and then eventually to trying to decide how humanity and divinity can co-exist in one person. To some extent then, Knox's suggestion can be regarded not as innovatory but as a return to a primitive New Testament position.

Similar to Knox's thinking is that of Norman Pittenger, especially in *Christology Reconsidered* (1970), though he is also influenced by 'process' thought. He too wants to talk about what God was *doing* in Christ and not about natures, for to do the latter is speculative and leads to false problems. To a degree, this whole approach is akin to Logos-christology: God has acted and revealed himself in many and various ways, but does so now not through the prophet's word nor through historical movements, but through a human life. Talk about pre-existence arises from the fact that what God does in Jesus Christ reflects what he has always been; of course God's self-expressive Logos was pre-existent, but it does not follow that Christ was pre-existent.

This proposal has been somewhat complicated by the fact that both Knox and Pittenger regard the event as not just the life and activity of Jesus, but the whole matrix of events connected with him, including the faith-response of his followers. The 'event' is thus really Jesus plus his community, yet he is the central, crucial figure, and the dissipating effect of the 'constellation' (Pittenger's word) around him must not be exaggerated. There is a certain obviousness about this extension: if we maintain that Jesus reveals God, we cannot ignore the peripheral but not therefore unimportant agencies of the

124

gospel writers, the apostles, and the community as a whole. Jesus was no isolated individual but the centre of a movement, of a whole stratum of events.

Knox and Pittenger are not alone. The latter can with reason claim the support of Hugh Montefiore, Maurice Wiles, and D. M. Baillie. In chapter 6 of *The Human Face of God*, John Robinson argues in detail that though there are also mythological and ontological ways of talking about Christ in the New Testament, the functional is the dominant way, and the most useful for us today. Moreover, he says that to speak functionally is not necessarily to say *less*. Anthony Hanson in *Grace and Truth* acknowledges a debt to both Baillie and Pittenger, despite his criticism of them at important points, and his approach to the question is fundamentally similar to theirs. What it boils down to is that the divinity of Jesus Christ is what God *does* in and through him. There is no need to speak of two natures, for there is only one, a human nature, through which however God is truly at work and is truly to be encountered. God acts, thinks Pittenger, in the same manner in Christ as he acts everywhere else, which raises the question whether Christ is then any different from any other rather good human being. This question is raised by most of the suggestions we are considering, but we shall reserve any account of possible answers till the end.

The Divinity is the Humanity

This view finds varying expression and is often just an element in something more embracing, but it does have just enough identity to be taken separately. It has two main aspects. On the one hand, it declines to see the humanity and divinity of Christ in opposition to one another, for it takes God to make true humanity. On the other hand, Christ becomes the definition of what it is to be truly human – we do not fit him into an already existing definition. He pioneers and represents the humanity that is to be, that which is God's intention for mankind. He is future man, and true man. Such a view tends to be labelled a christology 'from below', i.e. one which starts from the concrete, historical Jesus of Nazareth, explores what he is and does, until it finds God in him through his humanness. The alternative is a christology 'from above', one which starts with a divine Being, the second person of the trinity, or the Logos, or simply God, and then proceeds to discover how such a Being becomes man. Karl Barth is perhaps the most famous exponent 'from above'. W. Pannenberg in *Jesus God and Man* argues for an approach 'from below' and for him the divinity of Christ lies not in any 'nature', but in the Father–Son relationship and in Jesus' total dedication to the Father, by which he participates in the Father's being. This does not clash with his true humanity, for in being the revelation of God, and thus as Pannenberg thinks divine, he is also the revelation of man as he is intended and destined to be by God.

Whether the 'from above/below' debate is a useful contribution to the discussion is questionable. It does locate the starting-point of any given christology, but in a world-view which finds God 'all the way through', as Pittenger puts it, the distinction loses its edge. The terms unfortunately can become merely abusive, so that 'from below' is taken to mean 'reductionist', another theological term of abuse, and 'from above' is taken to imply a God who visits a world and its inhabitants from which he has hitherto been absent.

The idea that Jesus is future man has good New Testament support. Christ as the last Adam represents man's final condition, and if, as Pannenberg holds, we ought to view what things have been and now are in the light of what they will finally be, then it is plausible to say that what seems now to be anomalous is in fact the normal of the future. Yet even many who do not work so firmly from the future, find it fruitful to maintain that it takes God to show what true humanness is, and that thus the humanity and divinity of Christ are not only compatible, but in their compatibility are a paradigm for us. In many ways John Robinson's stimulating *The Human Face of God* belongs to this last category, as does the more recent *Grace and Truth* of Anthony Hanson. The basic unwillingness, in this approach, to see divinity and humanity as ultimately in opposition or competition leads us directly into the next suggestion.

Complementary Humanity and Divinity

Something that others have perhaps been feeling after, comes to full and explicit expression in the writing of the Dutch Jesuit, Piet Schoonenberg (see *The Christ*, 1972). He claims that there is a basic mistake about categories in much thinking about Christ, a mistake which leads to many of the well-known problems. When we talk about the person of Christ, we too readily slip into letting the 'humanity' and the 'divinity' jostle for position, as if they were competitors both of whom have to be somehow accommodated almost on the same level in the one person. It is the same when we talk about God's action in the created world and in history: God's action and human action are seen as competitors or alternatives – *either* God did it, *or* man did it. Schoonenberg argues that this is a false and misleading dichotomy. To say that God did Y, and to say that man did Y, need not be two competing statements, but two equally true statements from different standpoints and on different levels about the same thing. Did God heal me from pneumonia, or did antibiotics? The choice cannot be made for both are true. This is because God's action is fundamentally not across normal causality, human wills and human decisions, but through them. To say that I did X, purely within my own physical and mental capacities, and of my own volition, and to say that God did the same X, is by no means contradictory, for it is precisely through the natural, the ordinary, and the human that God normally works.

God is he who enables everything to be what it is (a point we have noticed several times) whether we are thinking of objects or persons. *This includes enabling my actions, thoughts, and choices to be genuinely my own;* this point is absolutely crucial. It is not that God controls or supersedes my decisions and so on, so that I think they are mine though they are really being manipulated by God, but that my

127

genuine freedom, my character, my personality, and all my decisions can be mine only because God enables them to be so. This is what it means for there to be a God; he does not threaten man's humanness or freedom or integrity – he guarantees them!

In the second half of *The Christ* Schoonenberg deals with the question of the divinity and humanity of Christ, and here he shows that to say that Jesus is human and also divine is not self-contradictory, because the two statements are not on the same level (we saw that one of the weaknesses of Chalcedon is that it tended to give the impression that they are). It is not possible for a circle also to be a square, for both are different entities in the same category of geometric figures, and to be one by definition excludes being the other. But for a human being to be divine is not in the same way impossible, for God and man are not in the same category as comparable beings, and God is he who enables man to be man. In a penetrating criticism of *Myth* Herbert McCabe argues that the symposiasts reject a doctrine of the incarnation based on an inadequate view of God, inadequate just at this point. They assume, he says, that 'God' and 'man' are comparable terms and must play the same *kind* of role in the one person Jesus Christ. McCabe argues on the contrary that the meaning of 'man' does not exclude 'God' in the way that the meaning of 'square' excludes 'circle'. We are back with our familiar point that God is not just one more item or entity in the universe. To say that Christ is human and divine is not like saying a circle is square, because the divine is what enables human to be human (and the circle a circle and so on).

This does not mean that we can easily call a man divine, but it does mean that the problem is not exaggerated by a false logic. Now Schoonenberg argues that God was not just active but present in Jesus Christ. Jesus was in every way a complete human being, with a human mind and will, human knowledge and experience, who made human decisions. We can in Robinson's terms tell a human story about him. Yet we can also tell a divine story about him, not so as to detract from or modify the human one, but so as to interpret it, see it on a different level. (Robinson wrote *The Human Face of God* before reading *The Christ*, but in a footnote on p. 109 gives a very enthusiastic welcome to Schoonenberg's exposition.) The two stories are complementary because divinity and humanity are not in competition. God's presence in Jesus is not, however, as a person. There are not two natures to be reconciled nor of course two persons, God and Jesus, to be accommodated, but only one nature and one person, the man Jesus. God is present in Jesus *in* his humanity, and not by adding something else. To use Johannine language, the Logos (Word) of God, his self-communication, was just that and not a person, until expressed in Christ. For those interested in the traditional terminology, Schoonenberg reverses the ancient suggestion and sees not the humanity but the divinity as anhypostatic (i.e. lacking a personal centre).

Even this sketchy introduction may suggest some similarities with D. M. Baillie's *God Was in Christ* and its stress on 'the paradox of grace' as a model for understanding the divine and human in Christ (see his chapter 15). It is also clearly compatible with Robinson's insistence that in (for example) Hebrews there can be both very lofty christology indeed and also a thoroughly human Jesus who has to overcome temptation, precisely because the lofty christology does not compete with the human story but interprets it on a different level. How far this sort of solution replaces the Chalcedonian, and how far it translates it, is a matter for debate, but certainly it offers an account of incarnation that cannot be easily dismissed. Moreover, it does preserve what Chalcedon aimed to safeguard: the divinity, the humanity, and the unity of Christ. Of course critics will ask how far this theory makes Jesus any different from any other good person, but this question we must once again defer for a little.

Spirit rather than Person

Some years ago in an article in the symposium *Christ, Faith and History* G. W. H. Lampe sketched out a 'Spirit' approach to the person of Christ. He developed this into a full scale theology for the 1976 Bampton Lectures, published in 1977 under the title *God as Spirit*. Allowing for the different conceptual framework, his approach shows marked similarity with Schoonenberg's at some points. God *is* (and does not *have*) Spirit, and despite nearly 20 centuries of Christian doctrine, this Spirit ought not to be thought of as one person in a trinitarian God, but simply as God himself in his activity, his outreach, and particularly in his outreach towards man. This, if taken seriously, has innumerable consequences in almost every area of theology, especially in the doctrine of God, but we must here limit discussion to its consequences for christology.

God as Spirit is always and everywhere at work in the world and in men and women. It would be inappropriate to speak of his breaking into human history, for that would imply that he had previously been absent, nor would it be right to speak of his coming to human beings, for that would also imply his previous absence. There is nothing strange about his being *in* and acting *through* Jesus Christ, except that Jesus provides the focal instance of and key to God's dealings with the world and with men and women. He is the paradigm, the model and also the pioneer and enabler of our sonship. God acted as Spirit in Jesus decisively and in unparalleled fashion, but this acting was in a totally human Jesus. There are similarities in all this not only with Schoonenberg but also with Knox and Pittenger, though they of course do not employ 'Spirit' as their category of explanation.

If we wish to speak of pre-existence, it must be not of the pre-existence of Christ, but of God as Spirit who was present and active in him, and who is the same God who was in the beginning. In other words, pre-existence is simply about the continuity of God. Moreover it must be remembered that 'Spirit' refers not to God as he is in himself (which is beyond our grasping anyway) but as he acts towards and enters into relationship with us. Spirit as something extra, beyond God the Father and Christ, is a mistaken notion.

Christ's humanity is not threatened by God's presence in

him, because the work of the God who is Spirit is *always to enhance the natural* and enable it to be more truly itself. It is a misunderstanding to suppose that the divine operation requires the immobility and passivity of the inspired person. Now this Spirit-christology has 2nd-century antecedents, e.g. in the Shepherd of Hermas (see *Sim.* V vi 5–7), but of course as Lampe proposes it, it has revolutionary consequences for the doctrine of the trinity even more than for the doctrine of Christ. Unfortunately the notion of 'Spirit' itself needs a good deal of explanation and is not at all easy to grasp; moreover, we meet once again the question of how, on this reading of the matter, Jesus differs from any other good and creative religious genius. It is to this question that we must now at last turn.

How is Christ Different?

In traditional christology, this is the easiest of questions to answer: he is different in that he has two natures, divine and human, and thus is unique. The problem many have found with this is that he is too different, and that it is too difficult to maintain his genuine humanity. All the other suggestions we have mentioned, however, raise the opposite problem of how to explain his special character, a character which has been almost universally ascribed to him in Christian tradition and which radical modern theologians do not find easy to dispense with. They all seem to agree that the two-natures doctrine is not the only way to preserve his specialness. Pittenger uses the 'process thought' category of *importance*, in which one event in a series illuminates and explains what has gone before it, has a striking impact in the present, and provides the key to understand what comes after it. In this technical sense Jesus is *important*, for he is the one by whom all other actions and revelations of God are recognized and understood, in the future as well as in the past. He is the centre. This may not be convincing to those with a different philosophical starting-point, but it does attempt to account for the specialness of Christ as the revelation of God without imperilling his humanness.

Knox says that the uniqueness of Jesus was the uniqueness

of what God was doing in him, and Robinson too finds this an acceptable account to give. For divinity-in-humanity theories, Christ is not merely the prototype of the new manhood, but also its archetype and enabler, the one without predecessor, and this in itself makes him distinct from all others at the same time as it links him with all others.

For Schoonenberg, while God was in Christ in the same manner that he is in everyone, he was in Christ in a paramount fashion – for in him as in no one else we have God's total presence (p. 93), with a whole person penetrated, without resistance, by God. Lampe sees Jesus as the key to all God's dealings, the focus of all that he is and does. In all these theories, in one way or another, Jesus is granted to be special or unique or the focal instance of God's presence and activity.

Nevertheless it may well seem that we are left with a series of 'degree christologies', i.e. accounts of Jesus in which he differs only in degree, not in kind, from the rest of mankind; when this is said, it is usually meant as an accusation, a condemnation. Of course it is arguable that any christology by which he is different in kind from us must be one which fails to preserve his true humanness, and moreover that in a 'degree christology' a good deal depends on the degree, which may be very small or very great. It has also been said that if God's presence is basically the presence of love, then degree christology is unavoidable for there cannot be differences of kind in the presence of love. Finally, how far these various suggestions re-interpret Chalcedon, or by-pass it altogether, is less important than how far they fulfil its aims and intentions. At least they are constructive attempts.

Notes on Books

Introduction
  Myth and *Truth*
  J. A. T. Robinson, *The Human Face of God*, SCM Press, 1973
Chalcedon Re-stated
  E. L. Mascall, *Words and Images*, Longmans, 1957
  E. L. Mascall, *Theology and Images*, A. R. Mowbray, 1963

E. L. Mascall, *Theology and the Future*, Darton, Longman & Todd, 1968

E. L. Mascall, *Theology and the Gospel of Christ*, SPCK, 1978

N. Anderson, *The Mystery of the Incarnation*, Hodder & Stoughton, 1978

Event not Person

J. Knox, *The Humanity and Divinity of Christ*, Cambridge University Press, 1967

N. Pittenger, *Christology Reconsidered*, SCM Press, 1970

D. M. Baillie, *God Was in Christ*, Faber & Faber, 1948

O. Cullmann, *The Christology of the New Testament*, SCM Press, 1959

A. T. Hanson, *Grace and Truth*, SPCK, 1975

H. Montefiore, 'Jesus, the Revelation of God', in N. Pittenger (ed.), *Christ for Us Today*, SCM Press, 1968, pp. 101–116

M. F. Wiles, *The Remaking of Christian Doctrine*, SCM Press, 1974

The Divinity is the Humanity

W. Pannenberg, *Jesus: God and Man*, SCM Press, 1968

K. Barth, *Church Dogmatics* IV/2, T. & T. Clark, 1958

Robinson and Hanson as above

Complementary Humanity and Divinity

P. Schoonenberg, *The Christ*, Sheed & Ward, 1972

H. McCabe, 'The Myth of God Incarnate', *New Blackfriars* 58/687, August 1977, pp. 350–357 – see also the December 1977 issue in which Wiles and McCabe continue the discussion

Robinson and Baillie as above

Spirit rather than Person

G. W. H. Lampe, 'The Holy Spirit and the Person of Christ', in S. W. Sykes and J. P. Clayton (eds.), *Christ, Faith and History*, Cambridge University Press, 1972, pp. 111–130

G. W. H. Lampe, *God as Spirit*, Oxford University Press, 1978

Postscript

My aim has been to introduce some of the debates that go on about Jesus, without taking sides too often or too outrageously. Yet in the issues and writers I have selected to discuss, I have shown my own bias, and I am sure I have done less than justice to some conservative and traditionalist views especially by the small amount of space I have devoted to them. Brevity or even absence of discussion does not, however, necessarily mean that I think something unimportant: I have not talked about the differing christologies of the writers of the synoptic gospels, nor about the picture of Christ the liberator that one finds in books like J. Sobrino's *Christology at the Crossroads*, nor about the intricacies of the doctrine of the trinity as it bears on christology, yet I happen to think all these are matters of some moment. Alas, in a brief introduction one cannot do everything.

I have touched only the fringes of a vast, unmanageable and ever-growing body of writing. As I said at the beginning, it is fascinating that in an age of unfaith people seem to be under a compulsion to explain Jesus, or perhaps explain him away, and seem quite unable just to leave him aside. As long ago, he is hard to ignore, for he obliges us to decide, to define our personal position in relation to him. This leads me to what I suspect happened in the early days. First of all, people looked at him with Jewish or Hellenistic eyes and tried to slot him into their own ready-made categories, their own mental pigeon-holes, such as 'messianic pretender' or 'magician'. After a while, those who followed him found the tables turned, for he was becoming the point of reference, he controlled and constituted the pigeon-holes, the spectacles through which everything else was seen and categorized. In a word, he became their ultimate. We can talk about what is ultimate for us only in ultimate terms, and it is hardly surprising therefore that very quickly indeed they began to use divine language about him.

If sometimes we try to 'modernize' him and ally him to our other pre-occupations in the social or political realms, this is a sort of compliment to him: surely he must endorse what seems of prime importance to us! At all events, whatever our own theological position, we cannot ignore the fact that before dogma took over, before reflection and the making of systems set in, men and women of different cultural and religious backgrounds found in him someone to occupy the centre of their universe. All the questions about Jesus start from there.

Book Note

Jon Sobrino, *Christology at the Crossroads*, SCM press, 1978

Supplementary Book List

This list is limited to books not mentioned in any of the lists for each chapter, to books available in English, and for the most part to books published within the last ten years. It is merely a selection.

J. A. Baker, *The Foolishness of God*, Darton, Longman & Todd, 1970 – especially Part II

D. Bonhoeffer, *Lectures on Christology*, Collins/Fount pb., 1978

D. Cupitt, *The Debate about Christ*, SCM Press, 1979

A. O. Dyson, *Who is Jesus Christ?* SCM Press, 1969

C. F. Evans, *Explorations in Theology 2*, SPCK, 1977, chs. 7 and 8

M. Goulder (ed.), *Incarnation and Myth: the Debate Continued*, SCM Press, 1979

M. Grant, *Jesus*, Weidenfeld & Nicolson, 1977

L. Grollenberg, *Jesus*, SCM Press, 1978

J. L. Houlden, *Explorations in Theology 3*, SPCK, 1978, chs. 2 and 3

W. Kasper, *Jesus the Christ*, Burns & Oates, 1976

H. Küng, *On Being a Christian*, Collins/Fount pb., 1978, especially Part B, and Part C, V and VI

J. P. Mackey, *Jesus: the Man and the Myth*, SCM Press, 1979

B. F. Meyer, *The Aims of Jesus*, SCM Press, 1979

Lady Oppenheimer, *Incarnation and Immanence*, Hodder & Stoughton, 1973

K. Rahner, *Theological Investigations* I, V, XIII, Darton, Longman & Todd, 1961, 1966, 1975

J. Reumann, *Jesus in the Church's Gospels*, SPCK, 1970

A. Richardson, *The Political Christ*, SCM, 1973

P. de Rosa, *Jesus who Became Christ*, Collins, 1975

E. Schillebeeckx, *Jesus: An Experiment in Christology*, Collins, 1979

V. Taylor, *The Person of Christ in New Testament Teaching*, Macmillan, 1958

H. E. W. Turner, *Jesus the Christ*, A. R. Mowbray, 1976

B. Vawter, *This Man Jesus*, Geoffrey Chapman, 1975

M. F. Wiles, *Explorations in Theology 4*, SPCK, 1979, especially ch. 2

Indices

Index of Names

Allegro, J. M., 24, 37, 38
Anderson, Sir Norman, 123, 133
Apollinarius, 100
Aquinas, Thomas, 114
Arius, 102
Armstrong, P., 22
Augustine, 115
Aulén, G., 22

Baillie, D. M., 113, 119, 125, 129, 133
Bammel, E., 39
Barbour, R. S., 22
Barrett, C. K., 78
Barth, K., 121, 126, 133
Bartsch, H. W., 22
Betz, O., 22
Black, M., 50
Bonhoeffer, D., 121
Bornkamm, G., 17, 22
Brandon, S. G. F., 30, 33, 35, 36, 37, 38
Brown, R. E., 67, 68, 70, 78, 82, 83, 92, 112, 118
Bruce, F. F., vii, 38
Bultmann, R., 15–17, 18, 22, 44, 50
Butler, B. C., 120

Cadbury, H. J., 39
Caird, G. B., 65, 77, 78, 119
Carey, G., 110, 118
Carmichael, J., 37, 38
Carpocratians, 24–6
Chalcedon, 14, 56, 77, 95, 103–6, 108, 120, 121–3, 129, 132

Index of Biblical References